FROM CONFLICT TO COOPERATION

FROM CONFLICT TO COOPERATION

Succeed with Rocco's 4 R's

STEPHEN ROCCO

TATE PUBLISHING
AND ENTERPRISES, LLC

Published by Tate Publishing & Enterprises, LLC
127 E. Trade Center Terrace | Mustang, Oklahoma 73064 USA
1.888.361.9473 | www.tatepublishing.com

Tate Publishing is committed to excellence in the publishing industry. The company reflects the philosophy established by the founders, based on Psalm 68:11,
"The Lord gave the word and great was the company of those who published it."

Book design copyright © 2014 by Tate Publishing, LLC. All rights reserved.
Cover design by Anne Gatillo
Interior design by Jomar Ouano

Published in the United States of America

ISBN: 978-1-62902-019-8
1. Business & Economics / Conflict Resolution & Mediation
2. Family & Relationships / Conflict Resolution
14.05.28

This book is dedicated to my older brother Salvatore Rocco, who died much too young. He might be an unusual candidate for a book on conflict mediation because he often resolved conflict with his fists. But his regret was apparent, as he always helped up his opponent. He and his friends Johnny, Lou, and Joe all guided my hand in this book.

—Stephen Rocco

CONTENTS

PREFACE

"You can't"; "We won't"; "Why do you?"…such words easily arouse our back stiffening resistance with others. These are words that almost instinctively lead to conflict…conflict that leads it's participants with the "how did this happen" unhappy resolutions. What I describe in this book is regretful and not reasoned behavior.

I have written this book to peel away layer by layer the adhesive, almost primitive human forces which magnify conflict—conflict that can envelop co-workers and customers as easily as countries and courts. Its concepts can be used by participants trading real or symbolic elbows as part of our daily struggle to those conducting formal mediations or negotiations.

The uniqueness of this text is in the recreation of these same adhesive forces that can just as easily lead to cooperation between disputants. I have created eight vignettes that illustrate a range of conflict within society. They range from spontaneous conflicts involving police, and co-workers, to more formal disputes involving divorce and labor management negotiations. It concludes with the full divorce mediation.

In these narratives I examine how easily and tenuous is the descent from understanding to greater conflict among others. More importantly, I provide a step-by-step application of the ascent toward great cooperation. I call this application Rocco's 4 R's.

Not a rigid formula, Rocco's 4 R's help guide a specific awareness that the proper interpersonal pulse must be maintained with disputants. My narratives do not just discuss mediation theory – they apply it to real life situations. It shows how, when, and why specific theories such as reframing and paraphrasing are used.

My thanks to the thousands of families that I have been privileged to serve who are the foundation of my knowledge. I write that all types of conflict resolution – whether informal or formal – involves both art and science. I hope this book will help to provide both to my readers.

—Stephen Rocco

THE ROAD TO WISE CONFLICT RESOLUTION OUTLINE

I. **The Problem**

    a. What people "see": our own perceptions of events or people are the silent contributor to human misunderstandings.

        i. Even reasonable people are able to engage in unreasonable conflict given the human ability to misunderstand others.

        ii. Our own assumptions, biases, and stereotypes often escalate conflict by blindly turning inaccurate thinking into a self- destructive reality.

        iii. The more we act to prove something about ourselves, the more likely we are to engage in unreasonable conflict.

        iv. It is easier to judge a person than to listen to him

        v. Vignette grandfather and grandson automobile case

    b. People are reactive organisms, just as a person reacts in a defensive manner to protect himself from physical harm, we instinctively engage in defensive communications when we feel misunderstood, resisted, or evaluated.

        i. Man's fragile ego is constantly on guard to protect its self-image.

        ii. Our emotions are the oil that lubricates the human reactive engine, which ignites conflicts.

        iii. In conflict, behavior that is driven by our emotions is unreasoned and contrary to our own best interests.

        iv. The question is the perfect confliction tool to deescalate provocative behavior.

        v. Student grievance dialogue

    c. Escalating conflict is the end result of their human tendencies in which people blindly react to the person rather than to the real issues or problems.

        i. Man's capacity to turn his wishes and fears into a disguised reality prompts self-protective communications.

      ii. In self-protective communication the parties see the problem only from their perspectives, creating a biased and unbalanced view of the problem.

      iii. As a result, a polarized relationship evolves characterized by suspicion and self-protection.

      iv. The paraphrase is conflictual intervention that destroys self- protective communications and replaces it with better understanding of one another.

      v. Landlord/tenant exercise

  d. With proper awareness, either party can choose to stop this negative cycle of conflict and concentrate on wise and efficient decision-making for all.

      i. To replace regret with satisfaction in our conflictual encounters requires self-discipline, awareness, and goal setting.

      ii. The key to remaining in control of conflict is to let your adversaries believe that they are in control.

      iii. Rocco's—Four Rs provides a structured problem-solving approach to the wisest resolution of most conflicts.

      iv. Summarization is an extended paraphrase, which unites several conflictual themes into goals that can be solved together.

      v. Rivera/Police Officer

II. The Solution—Rocco's "Four Rs"

  a. Restructure the interpersonal momentum

      i. The direction of conflict is largely dependent on interpersonal rhythms that can minimize or maximize human differences.

      ii. Conflict can quickly degenerate into a negative free-fall when retaliation and unwise decision-making becomes the goal.

      iii. That same human energy that fuels conflict can be used to fuel cooperation.

      iv. Good negotiators bargain over objective needs rather than emotional positions.

    v.   Textile sexual harassment case

b. Read the conflict

    i.   Conflicting parties do not naturally move in a linear fashion toward wise problem solving.

    ii. Wise negotiators have to read all of the obvious and not so obvious forces, which motivate the conflict.

    iii. In order to "read" our opponents, we must first filter our own subjective ability to distort conflict.

    iv. Similar to putting a new frame around an old painting, conflictual reframing involves putting new words around harmful comments between disputants.

    v.   Divorce case

c. Redefine the conflict

    i.   Conflicting parties often have shared issues and interests that must be identified and reinforced.

    ii. A person's view of the conflict must be shaped by images that are in their best interests to resolve it in a healthy fashion.

    iii. Such images must demonstrate that a change in their thinking will result in a gain for them and not a loss.

    iv. Motivational bargaining is a method to help your opponent see your way of thinking

    v.   Student Peer Mediation Exercise

d. Reasoned, not regretful decision-making

    i.   A person's unreasoned reactions to his differences with others often prevent him from choosing the most reasoned of decisions.

    ii. Reasoned conflict resolution uses objective and not emotional evidence to resolve disputes.

    iii. Wise negotiators recognize that preparation away from the bargaining table is as important as action at the bargaining table.

iv. Communications that reveal the most meaning between people leads to the best agreements.

v. Community Group Home

INTRODUCTION

THE ROAD TO WISE CONFLICT RESOLUTION

Former wife: Look, you are not going to take your bimbo on visits with the children!

Former husband: Who are you calling a bimbo?

Former wife: You made your bed, now lie in it. You will see the children over my dead body!

Former husband: (screaming) You're not taking my kids from me! If you had been a better wife, this never would have happened.

Former wife: (bitterly) The kids hate you for this; they will *never* forgive you.

Former husband: And you will make sure of that!

CONFLICT! The word alone conjures up dark images of anger, estrangement, even violence. These dark images most likely resurrect unpleasant encounters with others, whether professionally or personally, in which we acted in ways unlike what we would normally expect of ourselves, in ways that left the best resolution of the conflict as a forgotten option. This is the type of behavior in which when we "calmed down" and objectively examined the problem, we regretted our behavior or at the very least, our loss of control over the encounter. On the other hand, we may have justified or rationalized our poor behavior as the result of our unreasonable adversary's "pushing our buttons."

The ironic aspect of the subject is that conflict with others is both natural and inevitable. In our close-knit world of human interactions, there is an inevitable clashing of real and symbolic elbows with other people. People have unique goals, objectives and needs that clash with others in our interdependent world. These differences may be as simple as two basketball players trading elbows as they disagree with each play's defense or two motorists arguing over who has the right to a coveted parking spot.

It may be as complex as two different ethnic groups fighting over divine land. Each group is guided by a spiritual hand that tells them it is their sole right to occupy it even if the cost is the lives of their young children. Or it may be a conflict as psychologically obscure as people polarized by unconscious needs to prove something about themselves. Managers trample on employees' rights, since they cannot be trusted to do the job right on their own. Disrespected employees then justify their own unreasonable responses in a tit-for-tat conflictual style that results in doom for the company.

For all of man's prodigious intellect—scientific, medical, or business ingenuity—he has a quite primitive response when it comes to handling conflict with others. When perceived to be attacked (either physically but more often personally), resisted, or evaluated in some way, he often instinctively reacts in a way that magnifies conflict. He has a unique ability to justify his own actions and minimize his contributions to a dispute.

He has an inaccurate ability to draw the worst inferences of another's behavior and the kindest self-assessments of his own role in the dispute. He fails to see how his adversary's behavior is often a reaction to his behavior. How else to explain fender-bender accidents resulting in otherwise congenial motorists trading vulgar insults or worse, lying in hospital morgues; family members seething behind slammed doors but regretful of wounding those whom they love; individually reasonable coworkers who let a small problem fester until each is oblivious to ulcers percolating in their bellies.

He has the ability to make unhealthy decisions even when he is aware that better decisions lie within easy mental reach. After a fender bender, the normally reasonable but now frenzied motorists get out of their respective vehicles careful to protect their fragile ego but mindful that little good will come out of the exchange. Family members, more reflective after their argument, question why they have to exhaust their ugly feelings before sharing the good ones; a coworker realizes that only his health and reputation are hurt in continued conflict with a coworker even if he is right.

This book has a very simple purpose—to help people negotiate their differences with others in the wisest manner possible. Wise decisions are defined as those that help people to remain in control of disputes when our all-too-human reactions are to act contrary to the problem's best solution. Wise decisions are emotionally mature decisions. Those decisions in which people accurately assess their own behavior as well as their opponent's behavior in order to make the best choices: ones that focus on the problem and not on the personalities. Wise decisions must be captured from those often ephemeral reasoned states in which individuals regret their act of patience to understand others: that small rational voice lying behind the forceful anger of the motorist getting out of his vehicle to confront his fender-bender antagonist; the realization that periodic family squabbles provide only temporary psychic relief and can create familial scars that may never heal; that divisive coworker squabbles often obscure their common interest—the viability of the company; and peaceful coexistence between countries may be as simple as each ethnic group inhaling the fresh innocence of their doomed children.

This book examines conflict in a unique way: it examines the human rhythms associated with both negative and positive conflict resolution. Rhythms suggest a fluid, changing communication process that can quickly transition from conflict to cooperation and back to conflict again. The text provides awareness toward understanding this vibrant conflictual system and provides specific techniques to maintain a positive and healthy problem-solving momentum in which all parties receive some gain.

Conflict's potential for destructive or productive rhythms are illustrated in a unique four-part process. It analyzes step by step man's almost instinctual capacity to magnify conflict and his descent to self-protective postures. It also offers a four-step model to restructure conflict when it inevitably erupts. With practice this model—named Rocco's Four Rs—is easily assimilated into a learned awareness that can sweep all conflicted parties toward cooperation and healthier decisions.

The common thread to all conflict—formal, international, business, legal disputes, or informal, often spontaneous conflicts with family members, rude store clerks, or coworkers—is people. Countries or companies do not engineer conflict, people do: people with unique perceptions, prejudices, or habitual responses that can blindly magnify conflict. This book is geared toward redirecting people's responses toward more mature choices that can be applied to all levels of conflict, from formal or informal one-on-one negotiation to third-party mediations. Each chapter focuses on one aspect of conflict and offers an illustrative or conflictual narrative as a working model to examine it. Each chapter concludes with one technical skill honed by the author such as paraphrasing, reframing, and summarization—by years of hands-on negotiation. The art of all good negotiations—the capacity to direct negotiations in the way you want them to go—will be enhanced for you in this text.

ROCCO'S FOUR RS:
YOUR GUIDE TO EFFECTIVE RESOLUTIONS

THE PROBLEM

A tired mother returns home from work to find her son lying on the couch and the dishes piled in the sink.

Mother: I thought I told you to clean the dishes. You're just plain lazy!

Son: Ma, I have an explanation…

Mother: Don't give me one of your explanations. I'm working all day to pay the bills, and you're sitting on your behind. You're not going to amount to anything that way.

Son: Right. You know everything. Maybe I'll just go live with Dad so that you don't have any more problems.

Mother: After everything I have done for you, you're threatening me! You'll end up a loser just like your father. So go ahead…don't let the door hit you on the backside.

Son: Thanks! (He limps out of the house.)

We can all identify with this unpleasant exchange in which mother and son offer biting words that probably neither one means. The exchange highlights the quick and predictive quality of people to release unpleasant, often misdirected tension. The conflict quickly escalates from dirty dishes to dirtier insults stained less by their real feelings than by their reactions to one another.

As family members, the "wick" required to ignite the mother/son conflict was perhaps quicker than less intimate situations. Once ignited, however, the defensive patterns resembled that of all conflictual participants: buttressed by one all-too-human amalgam of anger and blame, each party is swept along in a dynamic in which the most hurtful invective rather than the wisest solution becomes the goal.

From this unpleasant scenario, my four major conflictual themes can be developed that apply to all types of conflict.

The following are conflicts that can destroy familial or international peace.

A. What people "see"; our perceptions of events or people are often the silent contributor to human misunderstanding.

Conflict engineers its own special type of myopia for its combatants. Similar to the mother's first vision of her son and the dirty dishes upon entering the home, our views can be tarnished in complex ways. Depending on the length of her day's end traffic or the nature of her workday, the mother's reaction may well have been different. Her reaction then, may speak more about herself than about the dirty dishes.

The mother failed to see that there might be other explanations for why her "lazy" son failed to wash the dishes. The mother also failed to see how her own good intentions did not translate into good behavior on her part. Deep down she probably believed that her harsh words were useful motivation for her son. Perhaps her overreaction spoke to her own unconscious needs about her own life and losses. Regardless, she probably believed her son should be able to accurately assess her good intentions from her behavior. She, like most engaged in conflict, would be wrong. One human conflictual frailty is our inability to see how we might be contributing to the conflict escalation. We fail to see the interruption between our good intention and how our actions are interpreted by others. In other words the son viewed his mother's behavior differently than she viewed her own.

Conversely, the son failed to see that there may have been a positive explanation for the mother's caustic demeanor. He wrongly assumed her intent from her words, resulting in his own negative participation in the conflict. He contributed to the conflict's escalation by not considering the full dimensions of his mother's behavior—that she could have a good motivation for her concern. With that interpretation in mind, his own reactions would probably have been more positive and more reflective of her true concern for him.

B. People are reactive organisms, just as a person reacts in a defensive manner to protect himself from physical harm, we instinctively engage in defensive communications when we feel judged, resisted, or evaluated.

When under physical attack, our blood pressure and adrenaline visibly rise in order to meet the challenge ahead. Experts describe this jolt of energy as the "fight-or-flight" syndrome. Under personal attack—such as in the mother/son criticisms of one another—our physical reactions are as real but our responses more complex. Energy is directed at self-protective methods to protect our egos from harm. Unfortunately these instinctive reactions often lie contrary to wise conflict resolution. For in our desire to protect ourselves, energy is directed away from understanding our adversaries. In the end both sides are reacting to behaviors of the other side, which are largely misplaced.

C. Escalating Conflict is the end result of their human tendencies in which people blindly react to the person rather than to the real issues or problems.

The end result of the mother/son conflict is a self-defeating cycle of communication which dooms wise problem solving. As will be evidenced throughout the text this dialogue reflects elements that quickly envelopes most conflictual participants. Under a haze of self rationalizations, and often faulty beliefs, people often fail to see their own contribution to the conflict's growing escalation. They also misunderstand how this defensive cycle of misunderstanding cascades and builds to more extreme levels. Each side quickly join into a no-win system in which they respond to each other rather than to the problem. At the end of their rift, mother and son each utter words that probably neither means, but feel justified in uttering. Each is locked into a negative and selfish communication pattern that provides only temporary emotional relief.

The mother and son dialogue demonstrates that in unhealthy conflict the true issues got lost in "win-loss" terms. To resolve their dispute each party has to prove that the other party is wrong. In so doing, the problem loses all perspective. Each could have chosen to stop this negative cycle, but felt powerless to do so. Rocco's Four Rs offers instruction at every level of this cycle to turn disputes into "win-win" resolutions.

D. *With proper awareness, either party can choose to stop this negative cycle of conflict and concentrate on wise and efficient decision-making for all.*

I have identified some of the egocentric, self-protective, and emotionally charged behaviors arising from our differences with others. Given these almost unconscious reactive ingredients, conflict is likely to spin negatively out of control unless the cycle is consciously aborted. Neither mother nor son chose to clarify the value of their relationship over the insults associated with dirty dishes. When conflict is in such free-fall, insults often seem the better choice for parties to reflect on than their true feelings for one another.

The ironic aspect of unhealthy conflict is that more healthy choices often lie within easy reach. If mother or son chose to simply scratch the surface of their relationship, positive feelings for one another were probably quite visible. This holds true with many disputants—two fender-bender antagonists could be easily sharing coffee with one another if their differences were not falsely exaggerated in their minds.

Rocco's Four Rs offer a blueprint that uncovers and grasps wise decisions from unhealthy relationship styles. It examines and restructures the behavioral patterns associated with many disputes and unlocks responses that will lead to wise joint solutions for all.

THE SOLUTION

A tired mother returns home from work to find her son laying on the couch and the dishes piled in the sink.

Mother: I thought I told you to clean the dishes. You're just plain lazy!

Son: Ma, I have an explanation.

Mother: Don't give me one of your explanations. I'm working all day to pay the bills, and you're sitting on your behind. You're not going to amount to anything that way.

Son: Ma, I know you're upset with me. Sounds like you had a bad day, huh?

Mother: You don't want to know. I got a new boss who's driving me crazy. That is why I don't need to see dishes piled up when I come home.

Son: I understand. I wouldn't want to come home to dirty dishes with that kind of aggravation.

Mother: So, why don't you help me out?

Son: I was trying to tell you that I spent most of the day at the hospital. I twisted my ankle playing basketball, and I thought it was broken. I didn't want to bother you at work.

Mother: My goodness, why didn't you call? You're the only thing that is important to me.

A. Restructure the Interpersonal Momentum

Aha! If only all our conflicts were so easily resolved. The dialogue does capture a central tenet of this text that is part of all successful conflict resolutions. Its participants are swept along by wave-like communications rhythms that can magnify or minimize those differences. Sometimes that momentum can be changed by the slightest intervention by one side or the other. Unfortunately those parties have to be ever vigilant about cooperation's fragile nature. Those relationship-like open seas can become turbulent at any time—often capsizing the boat when the parties are close to a peaceful shore.

This book examines conflict in a unique way—it examines the adhesive forces associated with healthy and unhealthy conflict resolution. It provides structured interventions that ensure the parties will chose their wisest of joint options. For example, the mother and son dialogue reveals the parties' deep feelings for one another. While those feelings remained hidden in the first encounter, the son was resolute that he would not allow his mother's misunderstanding to harm their relationship. By acknowledging and normalizing his mother's feelings, he changed the tempo of the dialogue. The mother revealed her true feelings, which existed even in her first encounter with her son.

Many conflicts are far more complicated than this family spat at the home. The need to understand the malleable forces that make up the conflictual dynamic are always present, however. Many disputes begin with small misunderstandings that quickly metastasize to unrecognizable, out-of-control conflict. The Palestinians and Israelis will hopefully participate in a journey in which their common interests overcome their cancerlike behaviors. For instance, their common economic goals can result in tangible gains such as better homes and schools. That journey will hopefully begin with small positive acts and build into a momentum of greater trust and understanding of one another.

B. Read the Conflict

In any conflictual dynamic, each side is responding to two different realities. They are responding to what they see and hear from their opponents. Their beliefs are also affected by how they experience that reality. In other words, a part of themselves is involved in their assessment of the conflict. This inner reality—their current emotional state, expectations, assumptions, or wishes—can distort this outer reality. In the second example of the mother/son scenario, we see how the mother's displaced anger and false assumptions negatively impacted her reaction to their household problems.

To "read" any conflict, each side has to be helped to view their dispute in objectives terms. This means examining one's own inner state to see if their experience is affecting the goal of wise decision-making. In this example, the son did not act on his angry impulse regarding his mother's provocative behavior. He considered that she was acting atypically because of some unusual stress. His simple deflection of her attack quickly led to her powerful statement of concern for him. This highlights a second aspect of reading conflict. Our opponents often have to be helped to make wise decisions when their role is to accentuate differences. The good mother's false expectations that "good sons" clean the dishes for their tired moms led her to justify her own negative behavior.

In another type of conflict, a labor negotiator may harbor a wish that management wants to "break the union." This wish may reflect on personal needs for power or control or reflect a more generalized wish to confront management's past behavior of limiting some hard-won benefits. Labor's views on management's behavior may be right or wrong. The more their decisions for their representatives are made on evidence and not expectations, the wiser will be their decision. Unfortunately man's capacity to react to internal stimuli may affect their process. Ideally, labor would allow themselves to be led on a special mission to reassess their positions stressing needs to quantify and qualify their views. What specific acts of management convinces you that their goals have a sinister purpose? How much did these acts cost labor? How does this company's benefit package compare with other companies in their industry?

As two accountants sit side by side and use logic and research to solve a complex financial problem, wise conflict resolution requires a similar discipline. It requires a commitment to make the most efficient decisions free from exaggerated inner needs.

C. Redefine the Dispute

A person's behavior as a result of his differences with others often assumes habitual reflex-like patterns. For example, the mother's anger probably grew from her belief that her "lazy" son should appreciate all of her hard work. In his case, however, that inner voice that gave her permission to release that anger was not successful. She was guilty of not opening her mind to the other reasonable possibilities that explained the dirty dishes, a failure that plagues many conflicts.

In similar ways people may take equally strong but self-limiting positions in their conflicts with others. They may assess that a good boss or a competent sales clerk or a fair landlord would behave in a certain manner. These beliefs may reflect less on reality, however, than on their own underlying personalities, emotional needs, or even their own immature thinking.

People often rigidly adhere to these beliefs even when disconfirming evidence exists that they may be wrong. Why? For one, these positions often quickly nestle into their egos to assume a comfortable reaction that they are "right." For another, people often look to find a single cause for their problems. Their minds are tidy places: to simply blame their opponent eliminates the need to tackle their own contribution to a complex issue.

In addition, since these positions are so intricately attached to their identities, a change in their thinking would be viewed as a loss of some kind. People wish to avoid losses, and they don't want to look weak or indecisive.

For a change in people's beliefs to occur, the problem has to be "redefined" in their eyes. For one, they must become internally comfortable with a new position. As their identity-laden but often faulty initial positions felt right to them, they have to internalize and justify new positions. In healthy negotiations a person raises objections, develops arguments, and communicates his views to support his position. These very analytical acts ironically open a person's mind to someone else's point of view. For in making one's own arguments credible, he is opening his mind to other possible, more creative solutions.

The problem is also redefined as they come to view a change in their position as a gain and not a loss. A divorcing father may give up his eager pursuit for custody of his child if he can be convinced it is in that child's best interest to do so. His decision change is not a sign of weakness but one of personal strength, making the best choice for his child. This perceptual change in a person's thinking is not triggered by someone telling them they are wrong. It occurs because the person convinces himself that it is a better choice.

D. Reasoned, Not Regretful, Decision-Making

As stated previously, conflict with others is inevitable—it is a natural result of our differing and unique human needs and desires. Even with those committed to a joint search for the best solutions—who use objective rather than emotional evidence to support positions; who draw on precedence or expert valuation to solve discrepancies rather than might; who model trust and respect for one another rather than blame—that search can be a difficult one. In a "downsizing" economy, what is the right amount that allows the company to grow and allows its employees to pay their own bills? What boundary fulfills one country's need for security and the other group's need for housing? What is the best date for the tenant to vacate the apartment while allowing the landlord to recoup his rental losses?

For parties committed to this type of joint search this book will ensure that momentum maintains its steady course. For others it will identify even before they enter the conflictual dynamic what to expect. It will help them avoid the inevitable pitfalls that plague unhealthy conflictual interactions. For those currently enmeshed in conflict, this book will offer a healthy way out toward better decision-making. That way out can alter one's escape from angry confrontation.

Reasoned decision-making is emotionally mature decision-making. It is reflective, resourceful, and rational decision-making. It is decision-making in which you control the conflictual dynamic to ensure that the best resolution of the problem is made.

PART I

THE PROBLEM

WHAT PEOPLE "SEE"; OUR OWN PERCEPTIONS

Two men, normally non-violent, one a grandfather and another, a young adult, tired after a long day at the office and wishing for nothing more than a nice meal at home, engage in a spontaneous car episode.

Driver 1

Young Adult: Hey, watch it old-timer. (*Just what I need today, another old person who doesn't know how to drive.*)

Driver 2

Grandfather: Drop dead! (*These kids don't have any patience.*)

Young Adult: Drop dead, ha! Stop that car and I'll lay one on you. (*Please, don't pull over.*)

Grandfather: (pulling over) I'm right here, you creep. (*I can't let him talk to me like that.*)

Young Adult: (getting out of the car) You're a jerk. (*Everyone's looking at me. I can't back down now.*)

Grandfather: (also getting out of the car) So are you. (*Oh boy, now what do I do?*) (*Both drivers reflect,"What the hell am I doing?"*)

EVEN REASONABLE PEOPLE ARE ABLE TO ENGAGE IN UNREASONABLE CONFLICT, GIVEN THE HUMAN ABILITY TO MISUNDERSTAND OTHERS.

As we see clearly in this dialogue, conflict often escalates in a predictable, self-absorbed pattern of misjudgments between the two sides. Neither the young adult nor the grandfather intended to have a fight. Each believed that the other side did, however, ratcheting up their behavior to match the aggressiveness of the other side. In so doing, each side failed to see that the other side's behavior was reaction to his own behavior. To further this complicated irony, each side was a fair and reasonable person who simply wanted to get home.

Given the complexity of human communications, it is probably surprising that accurate assessments of others occur at all. In addition to powerful non-verbal judgments of each other, communication involves an intricate encoding and decoding process in which people try to accurately read another's intent through language. Cultural, situational, or emotional issues may play havoc with this filtration process, creating misunderstandings where none are intended. People are reacting to messages of the other side that are inaccurate.

For example, a prospective employee asked by his potential employer to define his best job skills, must simultaneously assess how he wants to communicate the intent of his message with the meaning he attaches to the employer's comments. He ponders: *Is this a trick question? If I sound too confident will he think that I am too pushy? If I appear too eager will he low-ball me on a salary request?* The employee's ability to make an accurate assessment of the meaning attached to the employer's communications may well determine if he gets the job at a fair salary.

In conflict encounters, a variety of factors contaminate the communication process. The true meaning of each side's intent is hidden by emotional overreactions. Each side looks at the problem from their subjective viewpoint, which lends itself to self-righteous, abrupt conclusions and blame. As a result these superficial judgments dictate that little effort is made to understand the meaning behind the adversary's communication. We then accentuate the faults of the other side and minimize our own contribution to the problem. We then fail to see that others could be misinterpreting the intent of our own communications, resulting in misunderstandings where none may exist.

Our own assumptions, biases, and stereotypes often escalate conflict by blindly turning inaccurate thinking into a self-destructive reality.

People's performed judgments, assumptions, and stereotypes about others distort reality and blindly accentuate conflict. In the automobile case, each driver had a preconceived bias toward the competence of the other driver based on age. This mental generalization created a reflexive response independent of serious thought about the episode. With such stereotypic thinking conflictual behavior is generated by this mental habit: *Old/young drivers are bad drivers; He is an old/young driver; therefore I'm right and he is wrong.* Convinced that they are right and the other side intentionally wronged them, no further reflection is necessary.

Generalizations have great value in our society. Scientific and medical technology evolves from valued theories that quicken beneficial research. Our ability to navigate roadways by automobile is predicated on our assumptions that others drivers will stay in their own lanes and stop at red lights. We gain judgments after years of testing such theories in the laboratories or on the highways.

Similar preconceived judgments about other people, however, often fail this objective testing. Some otherwise mature people form biases because of reflexive habit or underlying emotional concerns. For example, some irritated drivers "assume" that bad things—traffic jams on road construction—happen only to them. They take it personal when life presents irritations and look to blame someone for their anger. Thus the person who cuts into their lane or the slow store clerk who causes them a delay is viewed as someone who wants to harm them. In a similar type of mindset, many people carry philosophical assumptions that other people cannot be trusted or that they are stupid or lazy. Whether they are managers, companions, fathers or teachers such assumptions create a self-fulfilling reality for their owner because they view behavior through this tainted myopic life-lens.

Faulty biases play havoc with our ability to see situations as they are in real life. Should a company's business negotiator enter labor talks with an assumption that the employees should "be happy to have a job"; her attitude will permeate her judgment. Similarly, it the employees' negotiator believes the company is "greedy and uncaring" the labor discussions are doomed for failure.

People generally want their thoughts and behavior to appear consistent. If we like someone we have a tendency to interpret their behavior in the most positive way, even if that is not the case. If we dislike someone, we generally act in a way that will prove that this person could not be trusted.

Some describe the human ability to masquerade assumptions for reality as turning wishes into facts. We *want* to believe that our new physician is all knowing and competent since she will keep us healthy; we want to believe that the attractive salesperson is smarter or kinder than the average-looking salesperson, thus we give his or her product more credence.

The more we act to prove something about ourselves the more likely we are to engage in unreasonable conflict.

All people have certain psychological urges or needs that explain certain behaviors. These drives, often unconscious in nature, produce conduct that often is contrary to our best interests. Conflict blindly escalates because people act on resolution of their inner needs rather than on the reality of the situation. In the automobile case, we saw that each adversary had a need to prove his manhood and was concerned with the image of appearing weak. Ultimately no observer would have criticized a wiser choice to back away from the conflict and spend a quiet night at home.

Such behaviors are often built on mental defenses that we erect to hide qualities about ourselves that we do not like. The motorist's overreaction suggests that it is that very quality—weakness—that he had to hide with an aggressive veneer. Much of the violent, unprovoked acts we see in our society can be seen as emanating from this need to overcome general feelings of isolation, powerlessness and low self-esteem.

Salespeople often capitalize on these human qualities to stimulate purchases. A seller might suggest that the selection of his product would be a wise purchase. Only the person with doubts about his own intelligence would be swayed by such a technique. The person comfortable with his own mental competency is not affected by this artificial support.

These behaviors unwittingly trigger conflict because people see reality only from a skewed perspective. The business manager who believes employees cannot be trusted will harbor chronic suspicions of all their efforts; the male domestic batterer will see any acts of independence by his partner as a violation of his control of her; the country asserting new independence from a tyrannical despot may view any peace-keeping restrictions as an attack on its need to be completely independent.

It does not matter what the need is—kindness, assertiveness, toughness, independence—the more a person acts on this quality, the less chance he has to view a situation objectively. The conflict has less chance to be settled in a wise fashion as a result of this mental defense.

It is easier to judge a person than to listen to him.

How often have we stared at a person pretending to absorb his or her message when our mind was on the fairway of our favorite golf course? Depending upon your emotional state, that day's events, or whether you even like the speaker, our active mental state clutters the message to our minds. The speaker eventually realizes—through your non-verbal behavior, irrelevant questions or inattentiveness—that you are not really interested in his message. The speaker will probably also be irritated that you did not respect him or her enough to listen to the message.

In either spontaneous or anticipated episodes of conflict, listening is often conflict's first casualty. If we don't like a person's remarks or actions, it is easier to paint an interpersonal brush on the whole person dismissing him as "a jerk, unfit, or incompetent." Projection of our arguments, positions, or blame is synonymous with an expelling out rather than absorption in. We seek to "win" by force or our own agenda when in reality we win by drawing the person closer in order to understand him. The method or drawing a person closer to us is through the no-cost intervention of active listening.

Active listening involves the difficult task of giving another person's words, thoughts, and emotions as much consideration as we do our own. It implies that a person has to be comfortable mentally to reveal her full dimension as a person. It also implies that we should suspend judgments or evaluations and focus on the message of the communication apart from the messenger.

Active listeners not only observe the hair rising on the anxious arm of the speaker, but also understand *why* the hair is rising. By paying close attention to recurring, but subtle themes of the speaker, the listener attaches the proper meaning to the communications. Eventually, the listeners can accurately predict how the speaker will interpret events confronting them in their life.

Where conflict exists in our relationship, active listening discharges much of the negative energy associated with misunderstandings. Those who feel understood become reciprocally understanding of their adversaries. Those who feel respected enough to be listened to, work harder to respect the opinions of others.

Common sense dictates that in order to intervene in a dispute we must carefully listen to the other side. Listening invokes more than hearing what is being said. It captures both the explicit and implicit meaning attached to communications. It detects the mood, affective states, and non-verbal messages being conveyed from one party to another.

In this motor vehicle altercation, each side relied on the hearing of the angry words, the explicit communications, which justified his own unreasonable behavior. What each side failed to grasp were the implicit communications, what each side intended or really wanted to communicate, and use them to have a safe ride home. In order to grasp this deeper meaning, one side would have had to try to listen to his sudden adversary.

When we truly listen to someone we can more easily capture the more meaningful aspects to her wants and desires. A divorced wife might simply want respect from her estranged spouse before she will be more reasonable on the issue of his visitation with the children. Often people will bargain with someone in a manner that conveys that they want them to know how witty, intelligent, or capable they are. The adversary who "hears" that communication and flatters his opponent consequently improves cooperation.

Listening conveys respect to an opponent. People acutely realize when they are not being listened to. Those who interrupt, correct, or judge another person cannot be listening. They are forming mental arguments, which send powerful resistance raising messages to the other side.

Active listening is not easy. The human mind is an active one and our own need to speak creates a tension that propels us to speak rather than to listen. Eventually, however, most of those we listen to realize that we deserve equal time to discharge our own needs. Good listening by one side often breeds good listening in return. With these thoughts in mind, here are some key points about building your dispute resolution listening skills:

- Listen to both the verbal and non-verbal message of your opponent. Most communication is non-verbal (i.e., frowns, sighing, smiling, eye contact, etc.)

- Keep the conversational momentums going in the right direction with minimal acknowledgements such as "Uh huh," "I see," "Go on."

- Listen for central ideas rather than specific facts that explain behavior ("I can see you're aggravated about something.")

- Listen for what is not being said, as much as what is being said.

- Focus your attention on the message and not the messenger. Our own biases, likes, or stereotypes can contaminate our judgment of an adversary creating an either too kind or too harsh assessment of him.

- Watch their style of communications: use of words, (i.e., slang, vulgarity, attacking statements), directness of communications (i.e., direct, rambling, topic shifting), the credibility and maturity of their behavior.

- Pay careful attention to people's feelings about issues. Emotions are powerful motivators that often reveal people's deepest desires, (i.e., fear, respect, control, etc.)

- Assess the validity of the other side's assumptions, perceptions, and beliefs about the conflict.

- A good sign that you are listening well is that you can correctly anticipate their reaction to an issue or predict what they will say next.

PEOPLE ARE REACTIVE ORGANISMS

A Student Grievance Dialogue:

A college instructor, Ed Smith, has set up a meeting with one of his former students, Fred. Fred has threatened to file a grievance against his former instructor. The student alleges that he received an unfair grade and was treated in a disrespectful manner in class. Mr. Smith is astounded by the charge. He prides himself on upholding the dignity of all students and verified the accuracy of Fred's grade.

Mr. Smith: Please sit down, Fred. I've learned that you are upset about our class together last semester. Can you tell me about these concerns?

Fred: I hated your class! You constantly called on me and not the other students. You always said my answers were wrong. I worked very hard in your class, and I don't feel your grade was fair. If you don't change it, I am going to file a complaint against you.

Mr. Smith: That's ridiculous! I was very fair to you, as I am to all of my students. That grade will not change.

Fred: This isn't over. You were not fair to me. I'm going through hell, and I have a teacher who doesn't care.

Mr. Smith: I think you should concentrate harder on your studies.

Fred: (visibly frustrated) Thanks.

OUR EMOTIONS ARE THE OIL THAT LUBRICATES THE HUMAN REACTIVE ENGINE.

So powerful that they can strengthen or destroy families or countries; so all-consuming that they can trigger life-long behavioral patterns for good or evil; so mysterious that their existence is denied even by their owners; and so illogical that their owners may choose self-harm rather than to confront them– our emotions provide a rich, pervasive yet confusing aspect to human functioning.

One would think that such an important aspect of life would be better understood. After all, we can all identify with the full panoply of human emotions, such as guilt, anger, sadness, or joy. Yet we all have had an unpleasant emotional confrontation with someone and regretted our behavior. Even if we feel our position is correct, we need to recognize that when we allow our emotions to dominate our reasoning, we lose control of conflict. Not only do we often not satisfy our own goals, but the cost of "blowing off steam" is high. Wounded family members remember the perceived attack for longer than the legitimate issue that originated the conflict.

People are also vaguely aware that our emotions lurk within our psyche, ready to govern mysterious behavior at any time. The excessive worry over a decision that does not match that level of anxiety: the out-of-control anger at someone who is an innocent target of rage that boils within us, the angry and suspicious person who chronically interacts with others, with an "emotional chip on his shoulder."

Man has also adopted clever ways to protect himself from emotional reactions that he fears. The professor, whose professional identity is intertwined with his competency as a person, would refuse to explore a student's criticisms because to do so might chisel away at his own carefully protected ego.

So what can we learn about emotions—both our own and our adversary's—that will help us to reach a consensus with them? The origins of our emotions are as physiological as the hair that rises on the anxious arm and the face that blushes. We cannot control their eruption any more than we can control the nose that has to sneeze. Our individual emotions are a unique interplay of what is happening around us as well as what is being experienced from within. The bereaved understandably express their reaction to a loss through their tears. But their wish that others around them suffer from the pain that they experience often saddens and confuses them. People should no more judge the envy at others' good fortune any more than they judge the anger at motorists who weaves haphazardly in front of their vehicles. Emotions just occur—they are not voluntary. Obviously, what we can control is how we manage these emotions once they are unearthed.

This instinctual nature of emotions helps explain why we cannot predict how people will react to certain events. Some people react with anger to the inevitable roadblocks in life that others look upon with equanimity.

Our emotions prompt us to act first and think second. This occurs because our emotions are experienced as tensions, often-unpleasant tensions, which demand a release. The discharge of that energy—through yelling, hitting, or ideally talking—interferes with our thinking. There is literally no cognitive room in a mind that needs to spew energy out rather than draw it in. Once that tension is discharged, a person is more likely to accept the logic of someone else.

In our civilized society, people have learned that they cannot or do not want to act on their emotions. Certainly responding critically to a rude store clerk is understandable and holds no moral stigma. But where does the anger go at the coworker who wins a coveted promotion? Or the bitterness that is directed toward the elderly mother who continues her lifelong pattern of withholding affection? This type of hidden emotion—the type that unconsciously enters all negotiations—often puzzles adversaries who do not see the relevancy of certain arguments. These arguments have deep relevancy to the progress of the negotiations, however. Only when these emotions are identified and aired will the principals learn to trust one another.

In conflict, behavior that is driven by our emotions is often unreasoned and contrary to our best interests.

Wise negotiators recognize that all behavior is a unique interaction of how we think and what we feel. Our emotions provide a rich, if confusing, texture toward life, but all emotional decisions are not good ones. Similarly, our mental reasoning helps us to process information, but we do not want to make all decisions in a logical computer-like fashion. Few people would have children if they weighed that decision on a cost-benefit analysis. Our emotions provide true perspective on the unique ability to transcend tangible rewards for more abstract rewards of selflessness.

In any negotiation, emotions will enter the dynamic to either confound or ease the communications. This will occur for one simple reason—feelings influence thinking. In fact, in many of our conflicts, emotions will dominate our thinking ability. How often have we withdrawn from negotiations that had benefits for us simply because we did not like our opponents? Conversely, how often have we pursued questionable benefits in a negotiation simply because we trusted and liked our opponents?

Since we cannot ignore this emotional subtext in conflict resolution, nor can we predict what emotions will enter this arena, how should the wise negotiator handle this subject? Simply by allowing participants to release this energy through conversation. In our civilized society, its citizens have learned to discharge emotional energy largely by talking. All people have experienced the relief at sharing an intimate problem with a friend or sibling. While the problem may remain as severe following the give-and-take of the conversation, we feel better about the problem. Part of the satisfaction is simply the recognition that someone cares enough about us to listen to us. In addition, sharing our problem with someone releases the hidden fears and anxieties associated with the problem. Feelings that are suppressed, whether consciously or unconsciously, tend to magnify in importance. Discharged into the light of day through conversation, they are seen in a truer, more manageable light. Our ability to discharge our feelings through words is a safe, often more effective way to deal with our unsuitable human conflicts than through our behavior.

Given these human patterns, negotiations can be seen as a guided form of communication in which human energy is directed at identifying the parties' similarities with one another rather than to their differences. In the give-and-take of their expulsive dialogues, disputants ideally begin to see a bit of themselves in each other. That is, they become more respectful of their opponent's opinions because they have been validated. Respect breeds respect. There is a powerful reverberation when people begin to share their worries or fears in conversation. They recognize that their worries are not unusual. They also recognize that their adversary cares as much about their words as they do their own. This builds to the type of trust that is required for agreements to be maintained.

Man's fragile ego is constantly on guard to protect his own self-image.

People have a natural tendency to personalize their differences with others. From the student's perspective, he is not dealing with a fair-minded professor who may have mistakenly treated him unfairly in class. He is dealing with an unjust person when has mentally determined that the professor "has it in for me." In this student's "black-white" mental state, the instructor is dismissed as a jerk. All of the professor's actions toward the student will now be tainted by mistrust and suspicion. Such a defensive attitude can almost guarantee that the professor will fulfill the unjust role that the student has mentally created for him.

The professor has demonstrated a reciprocal human propensity. Prefaced by an "unfair" accusation the professor overreacts in an "I'm right, you're wrong" way. The student can be neatly categorized as a complaining and under performing student. Labeled in this manner, there is little need to probe the source of the student's frustration.

Man's fragile ego explains why legitimate differences between people broaden into stereotypical thinking. We all hold strong self-images about ourselves as fair, kind, or competent or other qualities that are especially important to us. Our discomfort is aroused when others seem to be judging these very characteristics that form part of our identity. People who challenge these qualities are seen as rejecting us as people. We can see how the professor reacted angrily to any challenge over his fairness as an instructor. His behavior suggests that he is defending his own ego from information that he may not be as fair as he thinks. A more secure ego could tolerate another's views and might even have to consider that the student has some valid points.

Whether by reflexive habit, past experience or to ease everyday decision-making people often develop broad generalizations in life. Such generalizations often allow people to predict and control his environment. In the human arenas, however, broad judgments—"older drivers are bad drivers," "female employees are complaining employees," "our enemy wants to destroy us"—unrealistically fuels conflict. Guarded and suspicious in advance of our meeting with this category of people, we generally approach them in a way that we can mentally conclude, "I knew I couldn't trust this person." In other words, putting people into categories does not allow us to measure the unique nuances of each individual.

Some of these reflexive prejudgments often serve to defend our own ego from anxiety. People benefit from having their thoughts and behaviors appear consistent. This is especially true when judgments about our own self-image conflicts with those of others. Thus the job applicant who does not get a particular job rationalizes that he wouldn't have liked the job anyway. To admit that the prospective employer may have had valid reasons to reject him is viewed as a loss in his self-image.

These types of rationalizations occur because of a process known as cognitive dissonance. This is a uneasy mental state—one filled with anxiety—where there is inconsistency between our thoughts and actions. It is often easier in our complex lives to make neat mental categorizations about older drivers, female employees and enemy countries, and act in a hostile manner consistent with those images rather than subject each person to individual scrutiny. Our own mental comfort is challenged with we have to acknowledge that we may be wrong. Our negative behavior would not be consistent with these new thoughts. To rid ourselves of this anxiety—this cognitive dissonance—we could admit our Fallibility: it is far easier to reflexively blame the other side for a problem's existence, however.

A Student Grievance Dialouge:

A college instructor, Ed Smith, has set up a meeting with one of his former students, Fred. Fred has threatened to file a grievance against his former instructor. The student alleges that he received an unfair grade and was treated in a disrespectful manner in class. Mr. Smith is astounded by the charge. He prides himself on upholding the dignity of all students and verified the accuracy of Fred's grade.

Mr. Smith: Please sit down, Fred. I've learned that you are upset about our class together last semester. Can you tell me more about these concerns?

Fred: I hated your class! You constantly called on me and not on the other students. You always said my answers were wrong. I worked very hard in your class, and I don't feel the grade I received was fair. If you don't change it, I am going to file a complaint against you.

Mr. Smith: I see, Fred. You believe that I was unfair to you, particularly after you worked so hard in class—is that right?

Fred: Yes, you seemed to call on me more than any of the other students. When I answered, you never seemed to think that my answer was correct.

Mr. Smith: What would I do?

Fred: You peppered me with further questions…like you were picking on me.

Mr. Smith: I wasn't aware this upset you, Fred. I want you to know that I think highly of your capabilities. I continually questioned you to stimulate your awareness to a higher level. Perhaps I failed in not telling this to you sooner.

Fred: (more relaxed) This is a surprise to me. How come I received such a lousy grade when I worked so hard for you? My parents are furious with me for getting a *C*.

Mr. Smith: I know you worked hard. This was a demanding class, and yours was one of the better grades. I think you are capable of even better work, however.

Fred: You do?

Mr. Smith: Yes. Why are your parents so upset?

Fred: I don't know. They are getting divorced, and I don't know if I can remain at the college.

The question is the perfect conflictual tool to de-escalate provocative behavior.

The question is a remarkable but often overlooked interpersonal asset to defuse conflict. A "window" to your opponent's mind, the question can be used to both give and get information. It can be used to stimulate new ideas in others as well as persuade opponents to reconsider old ideas. Questions can be used to gauge interest in a proposal, to clarify misunderstandings, and to generate commitments. Most importantly, properly used questions can immediately defuse roller-coaster conflict between adversaries who have not learned to trust one another.

We see the simple, yet effective power of the questions when we compare the two dialogues between college instructor and student. In the first scenario, Professor Smith did not consider why Fred had such a hard-edged anger. Professor Smith should have probably realized that Fred's anger was out of proportion to the incident. Something else was fueling this emotion, and the key to unlocking it lay with a simple question.

In the second scenario, the whole complexion of the conflict changed with the use of the professor's broad open-ended question. Once Fred's energy was discharged, the meaning behind his anger became clear. More specific questioning revealed that Fred was principally upset by both his parent's divorce and its possible effect on his status as a student.

Throughout this text, readers will observe the dynamic power of the question. It immediately stops in its tracks a negative momentum that fuels conflict. As in Fred's case the question reveals the more meaningful, deeper layer context to communications. Questions also convey respect. Your question reveals to the questioned that you value them. In return, their answers are deeply personal gifts to you. If you handle them aptly, cooperation will result; handled ineptly they will resist you.

In any negotiation the questioner, and not the questioned, controls the tempo of the dialogue. This ironic interpersonal aspect is crucial to wise conflict resolutions. Effective questioning—often as simple as asking, "Tell me what happened," or "What's wrong?"—gives the questioner the information to lead the conversation in the direction he wants it to go. Rather than unresolved conflictual energy going off in any angry direction, the query directs that same energy to the areas the questioner wants it to go. Hopefully the professor's inquiries stimulated the student to make good life-long decisions at a difficult time in his life. Compare the student's critical journey through the first encounter in which the angry student focused all his tensions on this uncaring professor. The goals of this interview became much different with the use of the proper question.

There are several distinct types of questions. Each has a particular function and purpose. It is important for the questioner to know when and how to phrase a proper query. Improper questioning can lead people away from the very decision you wish them to make. Here are three common types of questions used through negotiations and mediations:

Open-ended question: The easiest foray into the thinking of others, the open-ended question, is intentionally broad and easy to formulate. That is because in this type of inquiry the thought is in the answer and not in the question. In the above dialogue, the professor's initial request of the student, "Tell me about these concerns," is in fact a question. It's general nature makes it a very easy question to ask. On the other hand, the recipient of that question has to structure a response in a way that she or he sees fit. The recipient also has to organize those thoughts and clarify them in a way that the questioner can understand.

In the open-ended question, the negotiator is essentially prodding the person to think. These are excellent questions in negotiations, particularly in the early stages. They are easy to develop, they validate your opponent, and they provide you with information about your opponent. Open-ended questions often begin with phrases such as, "Tell me," "How," or "What."

Closed-ended question: The opposite of the open-ended question is the close-ended question. This type of question is restrictive in nature limiting those queried to a brief response, often a simple yes or no. In this type of question, the thought or structure is in the question. Thus the inquisitor must carefully craft his search, honing it to get the response that he wants. For example, a labor negotiator may ask management, "If we relent on the vacation issue, will you concede on the Saturday overtime issue?"

Closed ended questions have several uses in negotiations: (1) They are ideal for obtaining factual information, i.e., "What is the cost-of-living figure for this year?"; (2) they are excellent methods of matching your understanding of another's thinking with your own, i.e., "So as I understand it you want a COLA clause for every year of the contract?." Questions that begin with who, when or where are often closed-ended questions. They are asking for specific facts on positions. Remember, however, that their restructure nature can be intimidating for the questioned. Should they feel threatened by a request, they may prematurely reject an offer. Once rejected, people are unlikely to reconsider a valid proposal, as they do not want to appear weak or indecisive.

Prompts Question: As the name implies these questions encourage the continued expression of certain ideas by an adversary. Often they use the same words that your opponent used to draw out thoughts that are incomplete or confusing. Everyday utterances that people adopt to encourage others to continue talking are prompts. Examples of these are: "I see," "Ah-huh," "Go on." Such responses convey to the speaker that you are listening (hopefully!) and that you wish to hear more from him.

While a minimal appearing interpersonal technique, prompts carry great weight. The delicate dance by disputants normally requires some sort of comfort with one another. Prompts convey that the listener cares about the speaker and wants to hear more. Polite citizens have also been conditioned in our society to listen to another's viewpoint with equal vigor to how they have been listened to.

REACTING TO THE OTHER PERSON RATHER THAN THE PROBLEM

The following landlord/tenant dispute has been referred to a local community action center for mediation by the police. Their referral followed numerous visits to the home shared by landlord/owner and the tenant. The community mediator (CM) is seeing the parties for the first time:

CM: Good afternoon, Mr. Davis and Mrs. Jones. Thank you for agreeing to participate in this mediation. My function is to listen to each of you and see if there might be a solution that can solve each of your needs. I will ask that each of you be patient with me while I attempt to understand your views, which will require that you do not interrupt each other. I promise that each of you will get sufficient and equal time.

Our meeting today may last up to two hours, and we may meet again if progress is established today. If you do enter an agreement, we will enter it as a contract that can be enforced by the Housing Court. I am confident that the agreement we design here will be superior to an adversarial decision of the Housing Court because you will have the luxury of designing your own agreement.

Landlord

John Davis: (Interrupting the mediator) I want her out of my house right now! I'm sick of people like her living off of good taxpayers.

Tenant

Linda Jones: (Shouting) You rotten SOB! All I asked for was a few more days' extension to get my children settled. Wouldn't you want that for your grandchildren?

Landlord: My grandchildren wouldn't be living with a loser for a father like yours have.

Tenant: (Crying) My children have me now, you miserable pig!

CM: (Intervening) Folks, this is getting off to a very bad start. Neither of you are talking about the problem, but instead are focusing on each other. Let me understand why each of you is so upset. Now, Mr. Davis, tell me about the extensions you have provided to the Jones family.

Landlord: I've given the Joneses three extensions to get out of the apartment. They should have been out months ago, but they have come up with all kinds of phony excuses. My son has to live with his in-laws since he was supposed to move into their apartment. Can't you get rid of these jerks?

Tenant: Who are you calling a jerk?

CM: Let's try to solve this like rational adults, okay? I may be able to help you two to solve this problem, but first you both *must* stop all of the derogatory comments. All that leads to is more verbal retaliation, and a wise solution to your disputes is immediately lost. Will you both commit to letting me help you?

Landlord: I'll try.

Tenant: Okay.

CM: Good. Now, Mr. Davis, what I heard you say is that you're aggravated because Ms. Jones's move has been delayed one month and this has impacted on your son and his family. Is that right?

Landlord: That's right.

CM: Is it correct, Ms. Jones, that your move has been delayed?

Tenant: Look, I'm sorry that I'm not out of the apartment. Can I help it that my bum of a husband left me high and dry just when we were about to move into his sister's house? He's drinking all of our savings and now his sister rented the apartment to someone else. I go out every day looking for a place, but no one will rent to a single mother with three children under the age of seven.

CM: So you're saying that you want to leave the apartment, but that your recent marital problems compounded with the lost apartment, has delayed your move. Is that correct?

Tenant: Yeah, plus no one will rent to me because I have three young kids.

CM: I see, so further compounding your problem is the difficulty of renting with three young children. (To landlord:) Were you aware of the factors that have contributed to Ms. Jones's delay in moving from the apartment?

Landlord: I'm sick of her phony reasons. It's not my fault that she married such a loser.

CM: Look, I know you're upset, Mr. Davis. It must be frustrating not to have control of decisions in your own home. It seems however, that you have lost all perspective in trying to solve this problem.

Landlord: Look, I think I'm a fair person. I was always good to Ms. Jones and her children. I never complained when they were late paying the rent because I knew Mr. Jones was a bad act. But do you know I'm being sued by a former tenant because she said her kids were lead poisoned even though I deleaded the apartment! I'm trying to comply with the law, and five years later, she said I hurt her kids. She owed me hundreds of dollars, but I never even went after it because she was in a tough financial bind. That's why I want my son in there—to get rid of headaches with strangers. I wish I never even bought this damn house.

CM: Now I understand your situation better. You're saying that all your attempts to be a good landlord have backfired to the point that you wish you never even bought this house.

Landlord: That's right.

CM: (to both) Look, folks, from the little that I know of this relationship, it appears that you both have legitimate concerns and that you're both good people who are admittedly angry, which is understandable given some of your recent experiences. I think each of your frustrations is understandable. You have inter-dependent problems, however, which are difficult but not impossible to resolve with some reasonable effort. I think you both realize the benefits of solving this for yourselves. If you take matters into your own hands, Mr. Davis, you will be personally responsible for any damages, and Ms. Jones can stay in the apartment for months while this matter is settled in the Housing Court. From your own words, Ms. Jones, you consider yourself a good person who does not want this to occur—you simply want a good apartment for your children.

Tenant: That's right. I didn't know John had all of these problems.

CM: That's the benefit of taking time to really listen to one another—you both have difficult life situations to handle. Can either of you think of a way to resolve this situation?

Landlord: You might think I'm a bastard, Linda, but I really have tried to be good to you and your kids. I feel bad about this. Have you applied for Section 8 housing?

Tenant: No, I don't even know who to call.

Landlord: From all my problems in this business, I know a lot of people on the Housing Board. Maybe I can pull a few strings…

MAN'S CAPACITY TO TURN HIS WISHES AND FEARS INTO A DISGUISED REALITY PROMPTS SELF-PROTECTIVE COMMUNICATIONS.

In our encounters with other people, we often quickly judge or evaluate them as if these conclusions were based on hard objective evidence. To our later frustration however, we often find that these judgments are tarnished by our own false expectation, which distorts our gaze. We tend to act on our reactions of others as if we were applying the same laws evaluating people as the laws of science. We must realize that these judgments often reveal as much about ourselves as they do the other person.

We have all had the experience of meeting a congenial or an otherwise attractive person and instantly liking this individual. As a result of this positive attraction, the person may also have appealed to us as being knowledgeable, trustworthy, or competent. Perhaps to our later chagrin, however, we learn that the false images of that person were shaped by our own expectations. Psychologists would say that we attribute these positive qualities, even if they are not realistic, because we *want* this person to have these qualities. In human relations this is known as turning a wish into a fact.

Conversely, we have the ability to turn our fears into a false reality in encounters with others whom we feel are against us. To our later regret, we learn that the person did not possess the negative qualities, which we first attached to him. Again, our own life experiences and expectations help to fuel this out of touch skepticism. As a result, our judgments of a potential adversary are a byproduct of our inner reactions as well as the words and actions of those we encounter.

This fear-turned-fact human quality is often a major contributor to conflict. Prepared for a contentious litigation with management, a union negotiator may predetermine that the company cares little about employee needs. As a result, the union negotiator is accusatory and secretive in his presentation. In reality the management may harbor no such intentions. As the negotiations turn more turbulent, the union negotiator justifies his actions without understanding that his own needs have partly created a self-fulfilled reality. Reacting to his own fears, he also attributes the worst of intentions to the behavior of the other side. He may catastrophize the most benign words or acts by management or attribute the most malicious of intentions to their behavior. In self-protective descent ion, labor and management quickly fall into a negative exchange based less on objective differences and more on wishes and fears of each other. Before long the problem is lost in a mutual assault based on misunderstanding.

These wishes and fears are unique and may appear illogical to observers. They are very real and personal to their owner's and the damage they pose to themselves is remarkable. If we examine the landlord/tenant conflict we can see how these factors fueled the dispute.

In his own mind the landlord justified his anger; he may have decided that everything in his life would be perfect if he could just get rid of this tenant. He may have questioned why he is the target of bad tenants, a problem that no one else seems to have. He may have convinced himself that as a good father he should procure a good home for his son.

These potential mindsets could all be described as wishes that the landlord acted as if they were a reality. As a result he looked for little corroborating evidence to support his beliefs or methods to resolve the problem fairly.

This same false sense of reality also fueled fears that made his conduct more unreasonable. He may have begun to believe that he would never be able to get the tenant out. He may argue that people try to take advantage of him because he is a nice guy. He may be angry at himself for allowing this person to rent the apartment. All these fears magnified because his frustrations created an illusion that there was more to the issue than the tenant simply not having the rent. As a result, he was less concerned with solving the dispute and more concerned with justifying his victimization.

IN SELF-PROTECTIVE COMMUNICATION THE PARTIES SEE THE PROBLEM ONLY FROM THEIR PERSPECTIVES, CREATING A BIASED AND UNBALANCED VIEW OF THE PROBLEM.

Like hearing our own voices on tape or viewing an unattractive photograph of ourselves, we tend to discard the data that is contrary to our own self-images.

These normal, but quirky human qualities may explain why our inevitable differences with others expand to conflict. When aroused that someone disagrees or opposes us, we tend to respond in familiar ways to do interpersonal battle. Like a soft pair of comfortable shoes, we reflexively act on life-long feelings, beliefs, and perceptions about both ourselves and the world around us. People may lash out angrily at the first threat to their ego or simply deny that they possess certain unfavorable qualities. Even if these habitual reactions do not make us friends or achieve our own goals with others, they "fit" our psyche's need to protect our own interests. In other words our self-protective instincts can cloud our clearest judgments of the conflict.

Even otherwise bright or astute people are capable of the worst type of interpersonal magnification. The acts, motives and faults of our adversaries are projected in the worst way while our own behavior is sanitized. Anyone observing the dialogue of the landlord/tenant dispute would probably criticize each of them for being defensive and unreasonable. But each would probably identify himself as reasonable and the other side responsible for this conflict. How can we explain the myopic tendencies of people?

For one our ego—our sense of worth as people—is an inherent part of our own identity. When someone disagrees with us it is difficult to limit the dispute to one of legitimate differences. Rather, we are convinced that the person may be rejecting us as people. Our self-protective instincts go into high gear at this point. The landlord does not simply want his rent; he is uncaring and selfish. The tenant does not only have a cash-flow problem, she is evil-hearted and ungrateful.

This distorted portrait assumes bolder proportions as each side views himself as being morally correct. As this "I'm right, she's wrong" mindset evolves our problem-solving abilities are short circuited. People don't have to learn about the other side because they understand them so well. This type of internal dialogue easily builds to a victim status:

"Who does that person think she is?"

"She doesn't care about my needs."

"I'll show her who's in charge."

The dispute now loses complete perspective as each side mentally retreats to justify his own biased views. Hidden from reasonable discourse our wishes and fears, left uninhibited, exaggerate in importance. People now look to justify their self-centered views focusing on the words and actions of adversaries that will justify their views. Words and actions contrary to their own self-image will be discarded and overlooked. Since communications is now non-existent, each side only "hears" his own arguments and the adversary can not be judged fairly.

AS A RESULT, A POLARIZED RELATIONSHIP EVOLVES CHARACTERIZED BY SUSPICION AND SELF-PROTECTION.

This housing dispute highlights the human potential for conflict to spin rapidly out of control. Both the frustrated landlord and scared tenant have quickly decided that is useless to deal with such an unreasonable adversary. Their conflict, sealed in quick dry interpersonal cement, dooms their ability to see anything in common with one another. This unfortunate characteristic of the poor relationship is that each side's wishes, fears, and needs are often not that different from one another. As seen here, both the landlord and the tenant wanted the apartment to be vacated. The mediator's ability to help them see that and structure an alliance around this common issue will in large part, determine the success of the session.

All people can identify with the negative consequences of a poor relationship. Each communication exchange is painful as the guarded adversaries view one another with suspicion. While a good relationship does not guarantee the absence of conflict, a poor relationship invariably guarantees out-of-control conflict. People are not going to reveal themselves—their innermost vulnerabilities—to someone whom they cannot trust.

Common sense dictates that building a rapport with someone is crucial to their cooperation. People are drawn closer to those with whom they can identify. This does not mean that people have to share the same values or political affiliations in order to have a relationship. It does mean that each person wants to feel special, to be recognized and validated for his uniqueness. The person who takes the time to understand another person, even an adversary, reveals something very powerful about himself. They reveal that another person's wishes, needs, and fears, however different, are important.

As a result of this special validation, communications, the glue to all relationships become more fluid. As opposed to a discordant one lane communication roadway in the poor relationship, a good relationship resembles a ten lane interpersonal freeway. The easy transfer of information and feelings quickly encourages familiarity and good will between the two sides. People become more tolerant and less apt to misunderstand each other's intent.

The landlord/tenant dispute highlights both aspects of these points. Initially there was no relationship or rapport by the two sides. Each felt victimized by the other and naturally defended himself in an aggressive manner. Neither wanted to learn why his opponent had formed certain conclusions, nor did each want to explore creative ways to solve the problem. With the mediator's help, the parties began to identify with each other. As communication eased, each saw that his anger was not solely the fault of his adversary. Soon the parties' communications turned from blame to understanding. The parties then embarked on a different type of mission—to derive a solution that met each side's needs.

THE PARAPHRASE IS A MOST IMPORTANT COMMUNICATION TOOL BETWEEN DISPUTANTS, REPLACING BLAME WITH IMPROVED UNDERSTANDING.

The paraphrase is the most common, yet crucial, intervention that any negotiator must carry in his problem-solving arsenal. Deceptively simple in formation it immediately diverts people from attacking each other and corrects any of their negative momentum from building combative speed. Most importantly paraphrases build trust, not only between disputants, but in the negotiation process itself.

A paraphrase is at its simplest, a technique in which a person rephrases or restates the remarks of another person. It is equally effective in one on one bargaining or in mediations. In the landlord/tenant dispute, paraphrasing was the constant glue that redirected the parties' energies toward smart problem solving. Following the two sides caustic opening, the mediator listens to the landlord and states, "Good. Now Mr. Davis what I heard you say is that you're aggravated because Mrs. Jones's move has been delayed one month and this has impacted on your son and his family." That is a classic paraphrase, because it meets three criteria: (1) In a concise manner, it rephrases the main points of another's remarks, (2) It conveys the mediator's understanding in his own words, and (3) It describes, but does not evaluate the speaker's words.

Let's examine these three principles further. People with grievances are often difficult to understand. They may think that other people should know what is bothering them and tersely respond. Others may spout all types of relevant and irrelevant data that they feel explains their own behavior. Some may simply attack and blame the other side, but interspersed with their invectives, are legitimate issues which disturb them. Paraphrasing matches your understanding of another's words with your own. Rather than repeating everything that was said, however, it succinctly distills only the main points. This is done to eliminate extraneous or harsh data that will only complicate the issue as well as help the disputant to do most of the talking.

It is equally important that the person respond to the speaker in his own words. In other words, what the speaker's words meant to him. Why? Paraphrasing is not parroting back word for word what was said. It is designed to convey care and understanding to the speaker. It conveys to the speaker that his or her words are important and that they were accurately heard.

Lastly, paraphrasing is not designed to judge another's behavior; i.e., "Your father sounds like a difficult man," rather than "What a terrible father." It describes what has been heard and makes no evaluation of the comment. Its neutrality is what makes it so special. Both the speaker and listener hear the paraphrase and learn to view the issues differently. For the speaker, it is like a mirror is placed in front of him which may help him to reconsider what he said or the impact of his comments. For the listener, he is forced to listen to words of his opponent a second time, only this time it is without the insults or wrong interpretation placed on them previously.

The landlord/tenant scenario is replete with paraphrases as are all the scenarios in this text. This is a testament to their importance, especially early on in negotiations when suspicions and mistrust are high. Another example in the scenario comes right after the landlord's remarks. The mediator responds to the tenant, "So you're saying that you want to leave the apartment, but that your recent marital problems compounded with the lost apartment has delayed your move, is that correct?" Again we can see how the problem has been elevated in a simple way to one of legitimacy and not bad faith. Each side hears and responds to the problem differently after these exchanges. The greatness of these types of interventions lie in their subtlety. Yet paraphrasing is not easy. It takes considerable listening and practiced skill honing to say them in a way that both sides react positively.

STOP THIS NEGATIVE CYCLE OF CONFLICT

POLICE OFFICER INTERVENTION

A police officer responds to a call of domestic disturbance and observes a distraught young mother with her three young children.

Officer Robert Rivera: Hello, I'm Officer Robert Rivera. Is everything okay here? We have received a report of some sort of disturbance.

Mother: What the hell can you do for me?

Officer Rivera: You sound pretty upset.

Mother: Drop dead!

Officer Rivera: Hey lady, why don't you drop the attitude. Maybe I'll call protective services for these kids. *(After reassessing the situation, Officer Rivera attempts again.)* Maybe I can help the situation. Want to talk about it?

Mother: My boyfriend left me for another woman. Are you happy now?

Officer Rivera: I see. That must have been difficult for you. Did you two live together?

Mother: Off and on for several years. He is the father of these two children. He told me not to try to get support or he would finish the job.

Officer Rivera: Finish the job?

Mother: Look, I don't want any more trouble. I love him. I hate it when he leaves me like this.

Officer Rivera: I can see that you still have positive feelings for him even though he threatened you. I'm just concerned that you may get hurt, however. What do you hate about him leaving you?

Mother: The loneliness. He's not so bad when he's not drinking. He helps with the bills. Sometimes he gets mad, and you just have to stay out of his way.

Officer Rivera: So in the past you have accepted his bad moods because it's better than being lonely.

Mother: Look at me. Who would want me with these two kids? It's not so bad.

Officer Rivera: What is he like when he's in a bad mood?

Mother: He has knocked out some teeth when he's drunk. He doesn't even remember it. He twisted my arm pretty bad once when I wouldn't give him the house money. He's always threatening to finish the job.

Officer Rivera: Are you fearful that he might hurt you again?

Mother: He's never gone that far—although he never told me he had a girlfriend before. I just don't want to lose him.

Officer Rivera: Would you like me to help you get some protection, such as a restraining order?

Mother: I don't want that: he's always said he would leave me for good if I went to court.

Officer Rivera: Have you considered that it is not just you he will hurt?

Mother: You mean he could go after my babies? I don't think he would do that.

Officer Rivera: I have heard other mothers say that and then have to care for their children's broken bones.

Mother: I just don't know.

Officer Rivera: Look, I know I can't be here forever, and it's easy for me to tell you what to do. I am concerned about your family's safety based on the little I know of your situation. Your boyfriend's violence will probably get worse and extend to your children. I can help get you protection for them as well as some help from social services.

Mother: (Crying) Where do I get one of those restraining orders?

While the questioned may believe that they are in control of the conversation, we see that the questioner truly controls the dynamic. Through the use of multiple question types the police officer created a rapport, stimulated awareness and obtained a commitment from the woman to change her behavior. If he had "ordered" her to obtain a restraining order, she would most likely have resisted him. Through the use of normal give-and-take in a special type of conversation he stimulated the woman to make better choices for herself.

TO REPLACE REGRET WITH SATISFACTION IN OUR INTERPERSONAL ENCOUNTERS REQUIRES SELF-DISCIPLINE AND GOAL SETTING.

To respond to others in a problem solving capacity is not easy. People may be ill tempered, rude, and obstinate. While our immediate instincts are to cut-off, yell, or even punch out our adversaries, such actions exact a high cost. In this case while the police officer can certainly justify his initial response to this woman, consider how he will react later on if he reads about her death at the hands of her boyfriend. That sense of regret that he would feel probably inflicts the negotiators who have come so close to a peaceful settlement in the Middle East situation. Regret must be the catalyst for all adversaries to redouble their efforts at settlement when conflict's escalation makes it easy for parties to simply throw up their hands in defeat.

If we analyze the police officer-to-battered-woman exchange, we see that the police officer initially was not really reacting to this woman. In fact, he really doesn't know the full dimension of this woman's needs, wishes, or fears. She may be a quite reasonable woman acting uncharacteristically difficult, due to the stress of the situation. The police officer is really reacting to his own experience. Perhaps he is angry that she didn't respond as he would to someone offering assistance. His own ego might be fragile enough that he cannot tolerate questions about his competencies. He might be simply frustrated after a long, hard day on the job. The point is that he was reacting to his own experience from the encounter.

The wise negotiator exercises self-discipline to understand *why* his adversary is acting a certain way. For how can he hope to influence another person to change her thinking unless he understands that thinking? While it is easy to cut off someone who disrespects us, it is difficult to devote effort to understand the person's experience: What it must feel like walking in their shoes.

But that effort bears cooperative fruit. A simple acknowledgment of another person—perhaps just a validation that his anger or fear is natural and understandable—often changes the tenor of the conflict. Emotionally disarmed, the conflictual momentum can switch in a problem-solving direction almost in mid-sentence.

That psychological comfort often results in someone altering his thinking. In this narration, we see that the police officer did not try to protect the mother by forcing his logic upon her. While his protective instincts had logical value, they were not her values. It was only after the police officer helped her to confront her own fears—to accept a bad partner rather than live alone—that healthier goals could be supported in her mind. Free from the worry that she was not understood, she had to justify how her short-sighted personal needs were more important than her own safety and the safety of her children.

This police officer—like all good negotiators—realized what all good clothing salesmen know: a customer is more likely to buy a suit after he has tried it on. New ideas, like new fabric, must be put on, touched, and assessed from different angles before their prospective owner gets comfortable with them. People are likely to accept alterations in their thinking when they make new decisions on their own: slowly analyzing the pros and cons of the new thinking.

The police officer did not achieve his persuasion in a haphazard fashion. Like all good conflict managers, he realized that the true conflict largely resided in the head of the battered mother. Through his patient questioning, he helped put her fears in the proper perspective. Often people's anxieties magnify in importance if repressed. When examined in the light of day, these fears often crumble in importance. Through his goal-oriented conversation, the police officer guided the woman's thinking to a self-evident conclusion. She realized that the safety of her children was a deeper need than her feelings of loneliness.

THE KEY TO REMAINING IN CONTROL OF CONFLICT IS TO LET YOUR ADVERSARY BELIEVE HE IS IN CONTROL.

Wise negotiators realize that logic, like lost vapors, quickly escalates in the combustive chambers of human conflict. When frustrated or thwarted in the satisfaction of our own personal needs, our emotions instinctively arise to satisfy our own urges. Little listening, and less absorption of our opponent's needs can occur under these circumstances. Until these reactive forces are realized, people are generally unable to accept the logic of someone else. Those choosing to control the direction of the conflictual dynamic, help others to adopt the most socially acceptable avenue for releasing these emotions—through conversations.

Out-of-control individuals are often looking for the very thing that they lack—control. Their own behavior frightens them. Their inner anxiety has produced tensions that have overwhelmed their ability to make rational choices. Often a simple confirmation that their behavior is understandable under the circumstances serves to relax them.

The key to more relaxed and meaningful problem-solving discussions is the use of questions. Their qualities having already been described, they have an added value in conflict management. They give your parties a perception of control. In response to your question, a person has to mentally organize his thoughts in a coherent manner. To simply make a cogent response requires a higher form of reasoning than all-emotional functioning. This type of mental situation creates more mature decision-making.

In the dialogue we can see how the police officer utilized the question to both uncover the woman's fears and change her goals. We can almost envision her inner thought process as she was forced to confront the illogical nature of her responses. Her choice—to share what I describe as meaningful "gut level" disclosures—required that she trust the police officer. His questions revealed as much about himself as did the woman's responses. It conveyed to the woman that this special police officer was caring and intelligent enough to deal with the problems. In return, she revealed her important vulnerabilities to this stranger.

Rocco's Four Rs provides a structured, problem-solving approach and the wisest resolution of most conflicts.

Rocco's Four Rs provides a blueprint for resolving conflict—whether one-on-one negotiators or as third-party mediators in a wise and efficient manner. It identifies the human potential for maladaptive conflict as well as the subtle skills necessary to redirect those negative forces in a problem-solving direction. It uncovers and cajoles all of the cooperative rhythms that people inherently possess. While legitimate differences may divide people, bad faith and bad communication create a negative momentum that can further distort the problem. As a result, adversaries often have to be helped to understand that they are more alike than they are different.

Like skilled raftsmen navigating a long river, good conflict managers recognize that the downstream journey can be a long and treacherous one. Good captains smartly control forward progress in calm waters while vigilant for the inevitable turbulence at the next turn. Most importantly, their knowledge of the "waters" helps them to prepare for those hostile rapids that can easily capsize the boat. The navigator harnesses the waters own energy to steer it to the proper downstream goal.

Rocco's Four Rs work because it attends to your opponent's rational and emotional needs. People need to feel comfortable with their hearts and minds in order to develop trust in the cooperative process. This applies to spontaneous episodes of conflict as well as for formal negotiations. People won't swallow your logic, however strong, until you absorb them in some way. Acknowledgement of another's viewpoints conveys to them that this special adversary may be just smart and caring enough to appreciate their uniqueness. In return, our antagonists often respond in a more tolerant way toward our special needs.

Rocco's Four Rs digs beneath the surface of people's words to uncover the true meaning of their experience. As the episode with the battered mother demonstrates, all of these needs have to be assessed for a change in thinking to occur. These needs —for the mother, a fear of loneliness and low self-esteem—may appear illogical to those who analyze the woman from afar. Intimate identification of her needs as well as a redefinition of the problem in her mind was required before her behavior would change.

A SUMMARIZATION IS AN EXTENDED PARAPHRASE WHICH UNITES SEVERAL CONFLICUTAL THEMES INTO GOALS THAT CAN BE SOLVED TOGETHER.

Dispute summarization is an important problem solving skill. As a party or parties share their views of the problems and their feelings about it, the interviewer identifies both obvious and not so obvious themes shared by the speaker.

Conflictual parties may be anxious to have their positions aired and validated. So a rambling potpourri of issues may make little sense initially. Conversely as with this battered woman, speakers may be reluctant to reveal embarrassing or unpleasant things about themselves. Summarization is a skill, which unites bits of information learned about the conflict and the parties, and shares it in a manner that focuses on their opportunities for resolutions.

In the police officer/battered woman dialogue, an example of a summarization is seen in Officer Rivera's final comments. ("Look, I know I can't…"). We can see how Officer Rivera used the technique skills of the paraphrase and questioning discussed previously to help the woman. He patiently leads the woman to self-evident conclusions that her relationship with this boyfriend is a bad one for her and her children. The final summarization hopefully clears the mother's last mental hurdle to take a positive step and seek protection. His summarizations express his concern for her, his understanding to why she does not want to leave her boyfriend with self-obvious conclusions as to why she has to leave him. Thus the summarization ties in important life themes that become goals for her to act upon.

In this particular negotiation, the conflict was all in the mother's head. The police officer had to tip her internal weighing scales, in a way to help make her best solutions. If he tried to persuade her too quickly or too harshly, she would have resisted him. The summarizations delicately unbalanced the mother's mental equilibrium demonstrating the illogical aspects of her decision-making. As a tool summarization can be effective in any type of dispute. Three things categorize good summarizations:

1. **Timing:** Summarization is important after each side "tells his story" but also throughout negotiations. It monitors the progress of communications, clarifies misunderstand and ensures the forward progress of agreements. It should not be done too quickly or too often but at a time when parties are ready to receive important themes about the conflict.

2. **Content:** Summarizations should capture the central theme or message in the communication. While it should be specific, i.e., "I'm concerned about your family's safety" it should not be bogged down by minute details. It's designed to stimulate and clarify new ways to assess conflicts.

3. **Form:** As a form of extended paraphrase, summarizations should be descriptive rather than evaluative. Remember you are describing your understanding of the speaker's words rather than judging his behavior. Thus rather than Officer Rivera stating, "You must leave this man and protect your children," he airs his understanding that "It takes courage to leave someone you love."

PART II

THE SOLUTION

RESTRUCTURE THE INTERPERSONAL MOMENTUM

This is a civil rights mediation between a representative for women employees of a textile company and the company owner. The employees are prepared to file a gender-based discrimination lawsuit if a last-ditch attempt at mediation fails. They allege that a climate of hostility exists between female and male employees who commonly ridicule the women with sexist jokes. The company has denied a pattern of sexism exists.

Mediator

(M): (After setting the stage and inviting questions about the mediation process.) Perhaps we should begin by soliciting the specific concerns of the employees.

(E): We are extremely frustrated that the company has ignored our problem for years. They think it's okay to tell jokes with sexist and degrading portraits of women. It's a good company in some respects; we just want to do our jobs and be left alone.

(C): Come on, lighten up. A few women have even initiated some of these jokes. We take care of our employees—we have never had a layoff, and we pay our employees well.

(M): I clearly hear you that you believe your company is fair and that women have been treated fairly. Have you ever been concerned about some comments you have heard regarding the women?

(C): Oh sure! I guess if you take one or two incidents out of context, it would appear that inappropriate things were said. I just believe people are overreacting.

(E): Would you feel the same if your daughter was pinched or grabbed? We believe the men take liberties because an atmosphere of harassment has been allowed to occur.

(M): So you're saying that the particular acts would end if the company established a position on this behavior?

(E): Right. Some sort of policy statement that would establish the dos and don'ts of the company.

(C): I'm still not sure we have a problem here. We have a good, clean company. No complaints have ever reached this office.

(E): That's the damn problem. Your foremen ignore our concerns and laugh them off.

(C): Look, it you're not happy, maybe you should look somewhere else for work.

(E): Maybe we should just contact the newspapers about our complaints.

(M): Look, this is a very sensitive point in our discussions. Let's just look a little harder at the problems. It is apparent that at this point both of you have strong conflicting opinions as to what's going on within the company. It also appears that in many ways it is a good company. If the tenor of our discussion remains hostile and each of you carry out your threats, each side may lose, as well as the company. The people you represent have a right to have the best and wisest resolution as possible. Why don't we try to differentiate our misperceptions from reality, while you still reserve your rights to lawsuits or layoffs? (To the company owner:) How would you suggest we figure out what has driven such strong complaints by your female employees?

(C): I want to see the actual complaints. I still believe these incidents are open to misinterpretation.

(M): They can be complex. What starts out as a common joke may turn into an offending statement. Would touching episodes convince you, however, that some men may have taken it over the line?

(C): Yes. None of our men should be touching a female. I wouldn't want that for my daughter.

(E): Your foremen have several such reports.

(M): How can we resolve this factual discrepancy?

(C): Perhaps we should establish a committee of managers and employees to assess these complaints.

(M): Good. Anything else?

(E): I'll admit that some of these incidents may be in the gray area. Maybe some sort of joint policy statement by the employees and management could outline our position. Is this something that's possible for the company?

(C): Yes. We could also create some vignettes of typical examples that could describe acceptable and unacceptable behavior.

(E): If we felt the company listened to our concerns, we would not be so frustrated and angry.

(M): Good. Perhaps some of this was a problem with internal communication. In other words, your voice was not being heard by upper management. It sounds like this problem could be corrected by your suggestions. Let's explore some other ideas.

The direction of conflict is largely dependent on interpersonal rhythms that can minimize or maximize personal differences.

This text examines conflict from a unique perspective. It examines and restructures the human rhythms that exist in any dynamic in which people hold differences. When disputing people simply act humanlike—turning wishes into facts, acting on faulty assumptions, and overreacting emotionally—conflict easily spins in a direction away from good decision-making. A defensive spiral of miscommunication and misunderstanding cascades like a wave being swept along be a disagreeable wind. In the beach-crashed foam lie the remnants of the angry wave spent with seething resentments and often regretful actions.

Conversely, if properly managed, those same human rhythms can be used to enlighten parties to make their wisest choices. Those choices may be as basic as dealing with a potentially violent stranger on the street or helping the members of a small textile company to create a better work environment for its employees. These parties are moved by subtle airy-like thrusts that propel them, often unconsciously, on a joint problem-solving mission. Such an immutable process requires the skilled talents of an interpersonal maestro.

A wise problem-solving atmosphere does not just occur. One side or the person in the middle must understand that sound decisions, like a good orchestra, require a special type of reciprocated reliance on each other. People have to recognize that they often have to put aside individual needs for the sake of a larger common goal. They realize that the music sounds better when they learn to rely and trust each other and as a result they begin to see themselves in their new partners.

The beauty of this systemic approach to conflict management is that it massages the inherent but often well-hidden, common characteristics that unite most people. Too often, conflict-blinded people act on personal needs of revenge, power, or control, which have ephemeral, short-sighted goals. Whatever satisfaction a quick-witted insult toward an adversary provides, it rarely satisfies long-range goals to develop a sound visitation schedule for the children of divorced parents, protection for a battered woman or wise planning that prevents a sexual harassment lawsuit within a company.

Even bitter antagonists with divergent interests often share something in common, even if both only share the same sense of frustration. Attention to core human needs relaxes the process for the parties and makes them more receptive toward their opponents.

Let's examine how the mediator in the textile company case cajoled the proper cooperative rhythms to reach a consensus. Initially, the mediator established an atmosphere of respect not only for the parties but also for the process. The mediator's poised neutrality will often serve to elevate less-than-respectful past behavior to higher levels. In a sense she is modeling the very behavior that she expects to see in each side.

The mediator immediately conveys that despite their past experience with one another, this forward thinking forum will have a special mission. Each side will be acknowledged in a special way. Too often people fail to realize that each of us has special needs and urges that have to be aired and acknowledged. Like a tense muscle requiring relaxation, emotional urges also press for release of a similar tension within us. So powerful are these tensions that we cannot accept the logic of someone else, there is no cognitive room in our minds, until these pent up forces are released in some way. Mediation and negotiation offer the simplest way to release these tensions through purposeful conversation. We have all had the experience of relief following the expulsion of this often unreasoned energy from sharing a pressing problem with a friend or colleague. Our ability to better analyze the problem, to objectively examine it in the clearest light of day, often comes when this energy is dissipated. Wise conflict resolution can be viewed as a series of guided human expulsions. In them irrational energy is drained and more reasoned thinking is positively channeled to change human interactions.

Lastly, the mediator used his knowledge of people, specifically his identification of their respective needs, and redefined them as goals to be resolved by both sides. For example, the mediator helped both sides realize that despite their differences on the subject sexism, each cared about the company and enjoyed working there. In addition, this work was important to them in other ways (i.e., fulfilling salary, self-esteem, collegiality issues.) The mediator helped the parties to understand that these common goals—in fact the future of the company—rested on their ability to make more reasoned decisions. Any behavior that deviated from their common goal (i.e., insulting the women; angrily threatening to go to the newspaper) only hurt themselves as well.

In conflict resolution these tangible, obvious needs are known as substantive needs. We have seen previously how the identification of these needs, such as the creation of a sound visitation schedule for a child of divorced parents, gets lost in a conflict-ridden atmosphere. Refinement of these needs as goals to be solved by both sides helps to structure behavior around the proper mission. Behavior that deviates from this ultimate prize—attacking statements, topic changing, etc.—is easier to correct when a goal is established.

In addition to these substantive needs, people are also motivated by more obscure personal needs. Each of us wants to be considered special–we all want our thoughts to be respectfully considered and validated. In fact, in any conflict, the sooner an opponent can convey that he truly understands the other side's experiences and views of the problem, the sooner wise problem solving can begin. This does not have to mean that those views must be accepted, however.

Some personal needs are also unique to each person. One side may be motivated by needs for respect, autonomy, or control. Another side may be motivated by unpleasant personal needs for revenge, power, or jealousy.

The importance of need recognition is that all of them—both substantive and personal needs—must be identified before forward progress can occur. Even disputes largely substantive in nature—a company resisting a pay raise due to decreased revenues–often have personal themes. The company may fear appearing weak in future negotiations thus making their hardline position more steadfast.

Some disputes appearing substantive in nature—a police officer appealing to a battered woman's need to protect herself—may be due to personal needs. A woman may fear loneliness more than she fears abuse. It is only when the illogical nature of this need is aired by her that a better goal could be established with the police officer.

In the textile company case, we see that the women's group's personal need for respect was very important to them. Only after the company was sensitized to this by the mediator could better solutions be discussed. The company also seemed to be motivated by a need to control their subordinates. Perhaps they were fearful that this was the best way to manage this type of dissent.

The mediator purposely identified all of these needs and established them as goals for both sides to overcome. Soon both sides embarked on a joint mission to improve their ultimate goal of creating a less hostile, hence more productive company.

Conflict can quickly degenerate into a negative free-fall when retaliation and not wise decision-making becomes the goal.

Any negotiator or mediator must combat several forces working against her in order to build consensus with others. A person's tendency to retaliate against a perceived enemy rather than to understand him contaminates her judgment. Soon each side's satisfaction of his or her own needs becomes the goal for each side. The true substantive issues lose their priority status when anger replaces reason.

A good problem-solver helps to keep the window open to higher forms of reasoning. That job is a difficult one. At any time, individual reactive tensions and frustrations can short-circuit reasoned decision-making. Such a delicate job requires Michelangelo-type talents of an interpersonal artist.

In the textile company case there is a complex array of tasks confronting our mediator artist. The mediator had to educate and establish trust in both sides, who awaited her with suspicious eyes. She had to establish a tenuous rapport with both sides, deflate any of their faulty assumptions, and also attend to their overreaction. Not an easy task, particularly when one false word could tumble this shaky "house of cards" foundation.

The mediator succeeded largely because she was able to create what I call "personalizing the problem-solving atmosphere." That is, the parties had to be helped to see themselves in each other. This wasn't communication with the other side—management and labor represented people like themselves with hearts pumping nourishment for both their physical and emotional needs. Each had fears, wishes, and goals that made them more similar than dissimilar. Perhaps a symbolic light flashed in the mind of management's representative when he could imagine his own daughter being subject to unwanted touching. The stimulation and massaging of these images represent the artistic strokes of the mediator.

Let's break down this case, admittedly artificially accelerated, but useful for analysis, to visualize the theoretical ebb and flow of consensus. In conflict-analysis parlance, the employees initially presented their views in an effective manner. ("We are extremely frustrated...") Rather than attacking or blaming the other side for a perceived problem, the employee representative presented her position in an objective manner. She outlined her side's *needs; why* they had those concerns, and *how* those concerns impacted her representatives day to day. She also presented a balanced view that the company is a good one in many respects.

Unfortunately, the management spokesperson chose not to match the respectful presentation of his opponent. Why? Perhaps he was insulted that such a good company was subject to this type of perceived nuisance suit. He may have feared that his opponent would take advantage of a more conciliatory posture. In either case, he needed the help of a third party to reframe his comments or else he would talk the company into a lawsuit with this disrespectful attitude.

The mediator's simple paraphrase of the comments begins the process to higher problem solving ("I clearly hear..."). This accomplishes two things: (1) it distills the positive aspects of the remark, laying within the angry part, and (2) it allows both sides to see the problem in a new way. The mediator combines the paraphrase with a question designed to change any retaliatory momentum. Unfortunately, the frustrated women's representative objects to the negative tone of management and the problem-solving atmosphere declines. It culminates in a crisis type exchange, common to many conflicts in which parties throw up their blaming hands in resignation ("Look, if you're not happy...Maybe we should just contact the newspapers..."). It is now easy to accept shortsighted tensions relieving goals and not worry about the implications of the behavior of the company.

The disorder of the parties' relationships now requires the most reordering of the proper momentum by the mediator. Her summary statement ("Look, this is a very sensitive point...") captures the salient history of the conflict as seen in the most positive light. It stresses that the company is really nothing more than the human energy that drives it. The mediator captures the spirit of mediation in that there is "no future in the past." She points both sides to their respective responsibility to attain the correct long-term goals for all.

She then challenges them to adopt a mission to seek the wisest solution for all, unhampered by fears and false assumptions. That challenge is accepted immediately ("I want to see the actual complaints..."). Responding to urges to be more respectful in tone, management is soon swept along in an objective search for the truth. The employee is equally swept along in a current in which each side feeds and stimulates the other with reasonable suggestions. Riding the problem-solving raft the mediator can now simply be carried toward a joint solution that will benefit all.

That same human energy that fuels conflict can be used to fuel cooperation.

People are reactive organisms. As a response to internal and external stimulus the human body experiences tension. People ordinarily behave in ways to reduce this pressure that is often experienced as anxiety. Thus the urge to yell, control, or persuade an adversary emanates from this same physiological response to internal energy. How that energy is dissipated—to either understand, insult, or evade an adversary—is the focus of the discussion.

When conflict is analyzed, we see that some of each side's behavior is independent of the other side. Each may be responding to his own fears, false assumptions, or unconscious needs to prove something about himself. These inner tensions may motivate behavior that appears illogical to others. A need to prove one's competence or autonomy may propel someone to prematurely vacate the bargaining table where the wisest solutions still remain.

Our behavior is also governed by our reactions to those with whom we interact. When we come to trust our opponents—observing images of ourselves in them—we reveal important, often vulnerable aspects of our positions. Human energy is then channeled into meaningful communications.

Conversely, if we come to distrust our opponents, even when we judge them correctly, our energy is driven in unhealthy ways. Rather than being used to stimulate new ideas, energy is used to block fluid communications. The relationship is darkly defensive; information is guarded as suspicious opponents question each and every of the other's words and actions. The negative cycle escalates to self-fulfilling images that leaves each side silently concluding, "I knew I couldn't trust this person." Energy then is often directed at convincing the other side that he or she is wrong.

The energy required to close ourselves off from others is strong. It is so strong that it leaves little cognitive room for creative problem-solving. Thus the inevitable tensions that we experience are not geared toward wise decision-making. Rather they are used to block or question another's viewpoints.

Negative energy is also used to force one's will upon another. Since an "I'm right, you're wrong" mentality exists, a natural evolution of this thought process is to get someone to accept your logic. The failure of this approach is twofold: (1) logic alone does not solve most disputes, and (2) to persuade others requires an understanding of their will, rather than a breaking of it.

As is evidenced in the textile company case, the women's group required something beyond a new company policy on employee's rights. They also had strong needs to be recognized and validated in the right way. When their side received that type of respect, with the help of the mediator, they became more respectful of the company's position. This highlights the emotional component that permeates all conflict. All people require acceptance of some of their emotional needs in order for them to be cooperative with others.

Many negotiators fail in this strategy because they feel that if they have the stronger argument—a buyer who just has to accept the seller's "can't miss" logic because he has a better product at a cheaper price –business logic will dictate a sale. The negotiator's failure to understand the emotional underside to this sale, that the buyer could resist him simply because he does not like him, will continue to frustrate him. His failure is that of not seeing the problem from the buyer's perspective.

Too often, people seek to change people's minds by force or threats. Rarely does this last in satisfying long-term solutions. We again see in the textile case that threats to hurt the other with lawsuits or bad publicity only fueled energy directed at resisting the other side. No one wants to appear weak or retract from an established position. Their egos are now part of the problem.

Good negotiators recognize that one's will can only be bent by its owner. To be persuaded to do something, a person must become comfortable with this new thinking. She must internalize and absorb this new behavior, recognizing that something more positive emanates from this change.

In this case, the mediator restructured each side's arguments as a joint search for the wisest solution for the company. Rather than telling the women's group that they may be overreacting, the mediator employed questions and paraphrases that stimulated them to look at the conflict differently. Management was motivated to justify how such passionate complaints arose in such an error free company. Both sides' energy was then stimulated to consider the problem in a different way.

Good negotiators bargain over objective needs rather than emotional positions.

In most negotiations, opponents adopt a certain stance or point of view and bargain over those terms. In the above dialogue, at one point the women's position was that they would begin litigation or go to the newspapers if their concerns were not addressed. The company's position seemed to be that the women's concerns were overblown and they should simply go back to work. As we saw in that phase of the negotiations things did not proceed well. That is because neither side listened as to why each side had adopted those views. In other words, they had failed to understand their need, which motivated them to bargain in a certain way.

Good negotiators are aware of the basic interests that motivate people to act. They basically fall into two categories: (1) Satisfaction of physical needs such as those for survival, safety, salary, etc. These needs are often known as tangible or substantive needs, or (2) Those for psychological needs, such as those for respect, control, love, validation, etc. These more psychological needs are often known as personal or intangible needs.

We have seen in this text how the failure of parties to identify these important motivations has resulted in the escalation of the conflict: The fender-bender altercation (needs for personal safety); the unhappy college student (need for validation/psychological survival); the landlord/tenant conflict (lack of control). All represent failures to understand another's motivation. We also clearly see this in the domestic violence case in the past chapter. The mother's position not to get a restraining order did not match her family's need for safety from this dangerous boyfriend. Officer Rivera used his knowledge of human needs to identify that the mother's interest to avoid her loneliness was motivating her position. He used that knowledge to convince her that the safety of her children was a greater need than her lack of self-esteem.

Need-based bargainers recognize that several needs may coexist in any party at one time. For example, in the civil rights dialogue the women had a substantiated interest in feeling free from unwanted touching or suggestive comments. They also had personal needs for respect and validation from management. Until management acknowledged those personal needs, the group's substantive issues could not be successfully addressed.

Astute negotiators often use their understandings of people needs to control them. People who have needs to prove something about themselves will act on those needs rather than on the merits of the conflict. For example, a person who is unsure of his own competence can be easily swayed by an opponent who praises his wisdom. Sales people use this technique when they tell a hesitant customer that a particular purchase would be a wise one. Conversely this knowledge can explain why people will not act a certain way when they should. A person with a strong need for independence will leave a good deal at the bargaining table as a way to justify that independence.

How do we uncover people's core interests from their positions? Often a simple question, "Why?" will help reveal people's innermost concerns. Interest based negotiators simply unearth people's positions to find out what is really influencing them. However, people will not reveal themselves to us without our help. True empathy and concern for our opponent is a necessary requirement for that type of trust, as people will not reveal their vulnerabilities to someone who is insensitive to them.

READ THE CONFLICT

The family court mediator has just met a divorcing couple, Joe and Mary, for the first time, and has begun a discussion on a visitation problem involving the couple's two children.

Mediator

(M): Joe and Mary, my name is _____. I have been assigned by the court to conduct a dispute intervention to help you resolve, or at least look at your situation differently. My function is to help both of you make the best and wisest decision for you and most importantly, your child. To do this I must help each of you to listen to one another and understand each other a bit differently.

Before we begin this discussion, I would like to remind you that you have been given an opportunity to solve your personal issues. It is important, however, that you know up front that this is not a voluntary process, as the judge has referred your case to us, and he requires that we sit down with you and begin by gathering information regarding the issues brought before the court. If either of you feels uncomfortable with the process at any time, we may stop and decide what steps to take next. The dispute intervention is not a confidential process in that I may be required to share information with the judge and make recommendations, if asked. I also would like to ensure that you understand I am a mandated reporter with the Department of Social Services, and must report any concerns regarding the safety of your children. I don't know you or anticipate a problem, but I must make sure that everyone knows this up front. The judge and I believe that you are in the best possible position to solve and live with your decisions.

You will both be given equal time to speak. I must insist that you speak in a respectful manner, even if that is not your history, and try to speak for yourself rather than blaming and attacking the other side. I know this may be difficult, especially because the welfare of your child is at issue.

Let's begin.

Wife

(W): Look, you are not going to take your bimbo on visits with the children!

Husband

(H): Who are you calling a bimbo?

(M): Look folks, you have to talk nicer with one another.

(W): (Talking over mediator) You made your bed, now lie in it. You will see the children over my dead body!

(H): (Screaming) You're not taking my kids from me! If you had been a better wife, this would have never happened.

(M): Please stop. How are we ever going to resolve anything this way?

(W): (Bitterly) The kids hate you for this; they will *never* forgive you.

(H): And you will make sure of that!

(M): (Sensing a momentary stop in this confrontation) Look folks, the only thing I know is that both of you are hurting badly, and each of you is very angry at the other. I want to help both of you, but I cannot do so in this climate. I cannot change the past, but I can help you with the future—particularly if you want to make that a good future for your children. You have to make a commitment to me that you want to solve the problems yourself...or do you want the judge to decide issues like visitation for you? How committed are each of you to this process?

(W): For the kids' sake, I'll continue.

(H): It's worth a shot.

(M): Good. (Firmly) Please don't interrupt each other. Let me try to help you. (To the wife:) What are your concerns about visitation?

(W): I know Joe loves the kids, but he doesn't realize how hurt they are. Insisting on bringing his girlfriend on visits upsets them.

(M): That's the first positive statement I have heard either of you make. Very good. What specifically upsets the children?

(W): Although we have been separated nine months, the children still believe that we might get back together.

(M): I see. You believe the children are further confused when they see their father with a female companion. Is that right?

(W): Yes.

(M): Good. That helps me. So you are saying that one thing we have to address with the children is the reality that you will not get back together?

(H): Yes!

(M): How do you think it's best to address this "loss" issue with your children?

(H): Perhaps we could take them out to dinner together and answer any of their questions and fears.

(W): That might be too traumatic for the children.

(M): The children? How so?

(W): Well, how do I know Joe won't upset the children?

(H): Stop babying them.

(M): Mary, I know you have fears about this meeting. What are some of the benefits of such a meeting for the children?

(W): Well, at least they could see us as parents, and not enemies.

(M): Right. A message could be sent that no matter how difficult things might be, their parents would be there for them. You might want to consider that point. Joe, tell me about your views regarding your girlfriend and visitation.

(H): I started dating three months ago. I care very much about this woman, and I would like the children to meet her.

(M): I see. You want the children to meet an important person in your life, is that correct?

(H): Yes, plus they will have to adjust to my new status.

(M): So, beyond meeting this person, you think seeing you with someone else will help them adjust to the divorce?

(H): Right.

(M): What other kind of help do your children need?

(H): Well, I know my children are upset. I'm not a fool—but life goes on.

(M): So, I hear you saying two things. Number one, you want the children to meet an important person in your life; number two, you think that by their meeting her, it will help your children adjust to all of the realities of a divorce, correct? How long does it take children to grieve the loss of their parents' marriage?

(H): I don't know, but it would help if their mother did not portray herself as a victim—we both agreed to this divorce.

(M): I heard what you said about the victimization—let me get back to the "grief" issue. Could it be possible that your children—their particular personalities—require more time to adjust to their pain?

(H): Perhaps. I'd be willing to give them more time if it's necessary.

(M): About your perception of your wife... How do your children perceive their mother as a victim?

(H): It's not what she says; it's how she acts when I pick up the kids— she's so depressed.

(W): How am I supposed to act? Joyous? I'm not feeling great these days, but I never badmouth you.

(H): I'm happy to hear that. I just don't know what's going on with the kids. I miss them terribly.

(M): I'd like to commend both of you for your honesty and restraint. It's apparent you both are feeling your way through a major life crisis, and you have both acknowledged that things could have been handled better. That is a healthy sign. I see a hidden respect for one another. Let's utilize these positive forces to design a schedule that is the best for your children, okay?

CONFLICTING PARTIES DO NOT NATURALLY MOVE IN A LINEAR FASHION TOWARD WISE PROBLEM SOLVING.

As evidenced in the divorce mediation case the presenting issue for both parents was a suitable visitation schedule for the father. Specifically, the true issue under scrutiny was whether the presence of the father's new girlfriend was disruptive for the youngsters. The parents' distrust for one another initially served to contaminate this issue. Rather than clinical study of what might be best for their particular children—what their special personalities and needs require in their relationship with their father—this issue quickly vaporized in the angry recriminations of each parent.

In many ways wise negotiators must commence an objective investigation similar to a scientist studying a new disease. They must come with an open mind free from false assumptions; arrive prepared with the proper "tools"; test the functioning of the organism; develop a hypothesis as to its operational tendencies; and devise strategies that will arrest its pathology.

The divorce mediator used just such a clinical approach to study the visitation issue. In this case, however, the study of the "disease" was complicated by the parents frenzied anger at one another. The problem was lost in the reactive human layers of distrust and blame. The skillful clinician had to delicately peel away each of these complicated layers in order to have both parents focus on the proper issue—the ongoing welfare of their young children.

Most parties involved in a dispute cannot be counted on to move in a linear fashion toward their wisest choices. If that were the case these divorced parents could have implemented strategies themselves to minimize this tension for their youngsters. They may have called a family meeting and in a supportive environment encouraged the children to reveal their true feelings on the issue. The powerful symbolic message for their youngsters that, despite their spousal differences, they were united for the children's benefit is probably more important than the visitation dispute. As "scientists" searching for the best evidence, these parents may also have solicited the opinions of teachers, pediatricians, counselors, or ministers to help them make the best choices. Following such a search, the mother may have come to believe that her fears were unwarranted, that other issues confronting her children required more of her energy. Conversely, the father may have been helped to understand that his children were not ready for this post-divorce adjustment stage, that his particular children needed more time to "grieve" their parents' divorce.

In most conflicts, these all-too-frustrating human issues cloud each side's judgment. In the complicated fabric of our own personalities merging into the objective nature of the problem, reactive behaviors emerge that reflect more on the person than on the problem. For example, the divorce case illustrates that the father perceived the mother to be unfair and malicious. The mother deemed the father to be selfish and insincere. From these viewpoints, the conflict spun wildly away from prudent decision-making. Each side blamed the other for being unreasonable and failed to see his own contribution to the problem. Each side justified his own adversarial behavior as being necessary to "protect" the children. Each could not "see" that the other side's "poor behavior" was a reaction to his own.

For any successful transition from a diseased to a healthy model, any conflict manager must understand this human component to conflict. Parties often have to be helped to move to clinical decision-making. One way this occurs is that a negotiator or mediator serves as a model for the type of behavior he expects to see from others. Those who listen to others in a respectful manner often receive similar consideration back. Caustic or bickering parties will often elevate their behavior to more mature levels when a correct problem-solving atmosphere has been created. The road from resistance to cooperation is built by people who anticipate and understand how people will react to differences with others. They then create the proper interpersonal climate which enjoins all parties to search for the wisest solutions for all involved.

Wise negotiators have to read all of the obvious and not-so-obvious forces, which motivate the conflict.

A scientist-like conflict manager must learn to "read" the organisms' tendencies. After an honest self-assessment of his own goals, assumptions, or even biases, a person must make a similar study of his adversary. What appears to be the opponent's expectations? How does that adversary express those views? What are the individual's perceptions of the problem? Does the individual harbor prejudices or stereotypes about the other side?

What deeper fears or personal needs affect her behavior? Is this person emotionally mature (i.e., able to listen, accept criticism or consider alternate points of view?) How does the person see his or her role in the dispute or in its resolution?

Any mediator also wants to pay attention to the communication dynamic that evolves between disputants. What non-verbal clues does each side reveal (i.e., frowns, sighing, folded arms)? How does each side address the contested issues (i.e., direct, avoid, frequent topic shifting)? Describe the tone of the exchanges (i.e., hostile, defensive, integrating). Is the issue contaminated by personal attacks or unrelated issues? What is the parties' ability to move forward to a problem-solving model?

The divorce narration demonstrates that the answer to these questions often reveal the degree of the conflict. Initially we see that both sides were very angry and probably pessimistic that this special communication process could help them. Each side sought to protect himself by attacking the other with greater vigor. Eventually they used the children as a weapon to hurt their former partner.

We also see how faulty judgments about each other soiled the process. The mother firmly believed that the father's posture on visitation had a sinister basis. Rather than reconsidering that view, she assumed that he was selfish and demanding. Given this mentality, why would she relent on the visitation issue?

Equally as compelling, the father viewed the mother as using her maternal powers to sabotage his contact with his youngsters. With that assumption—turned—fact logic, he could justify any of his own behavior in this domestic war!

Underneath these self-protective veneers, the mediator uncovered that both sides had fears that explained their anxiety over the issue. In addition to wanting what was best for her children the mother also expressed feelings of loss and loneliness. Perhaps she was also angry and jealous that her husband's post-divorce life was better than her own.

For the father, he seemed fearful that he would lose contact with or control of his children. These issues of power and control may have been prominent themes in his divorce. His overreaction to the girlfriend issue may have been his dramatic way to prove his former wife could no longer control him. Unfortunately, his heavy-handed resteadying came at the expense of his children's needs.

As I have outlined previously, personal needs are present in every negotiation. The sports agent, the union negotiator, or the international diplomat all have needs, both substantive and personal, that require identification and attention. Some unique personal needs may be motivated by emotions such as jealously, shame, even hate, among others. These issues often complicate substantive negotiations because they seem unrelated to the tangible processes. In fact these intangible needs are sometimes more important than the issues on the table.

Most of these inner needs are psychological in nature and common to most people. Next to drives for physical survival—food, water and safety concerns—peoples' most innate needs are those for "psychological survival," that is most people have special inner needs for validation, respect and recognition. They may also be driven by needs for security, autonomy, or control. Each person wants to be recognized as being special—to have their thoughts and emotions uniquely recognized, however illogical. It was only when the mother in the divorce mediation felt appreciated that she could begin to appreciate her husband's views.

One cannot expect that all of these inner tensions will be readily acknowledged. Some fears may be barely conscious and they are often not flattering to one's self-image. It is much easier for the divorced mother to rationalize that the father is selfish rather than to admit that her own jealously complicates her decision-making. It is easier to bury these thoughts in her sub-conscious making them unrecognizable. Similarly, it is easy for the father to deny that his own need for control may force his children to visit with someone who further traumatizes them. Many over-reactive males in our society today seem to have a need to beat respect out of a disrespectful opponent. They fail to see that a self-confident person has no such need and his overreaction is a sign that he has a lack of self-respect.

What the mediator had to unearth was that these personal needs interfered with wise conflict-resolution. While satisfaction of certain personal needs relieve temporary tensions they rarely result in healthy decisions. The mediator has to create a safe enough climate so that these complicated personal layers could be surgically removed and the true "disease" examined. One false move in this delicate process—the wrong word or tone—could have a hemorrhage-like effect on the operation. The mediator ably created trust in the process by identifying the love the parents possessed for their children.

This good, reasonable side of most people emerges when they have become psychologically validated—respected, and recognized—which encourages them to treat their adversaries in a similar way. This healthy reciprocity also creates self-awareness that satisfaction of their personal needs cannot come at the cost of wise conflict-resolution.

In order to "read" our opponents, we must first filter our own subjective ability to distort conflict.

As people, we can only view other people's behavior from our own perspective. When conflict occurs, it is often easy to assume that the other side's experience is like our own—therefore what they want we are not ready to give up. We also come to honestly believe that our own behavior is reasonable and based on objective assessment of the situation. We patiently listen to our opponents; watch their actions and form judgments that ultimately affect out position in the conflict.

What many negotiators fail to see, however, is that our own observation can distort this objective appearing gaze. Our current emotional state, our expectations, and even our own wishful thinking often merge into our decision-making. For example, we may negotiate with someone and come to the conclusion that he is an unfair adversary. What we may be describing is our *experiences* with this type of adversary, that from our frame of life reference, people who act like this person are considered unfair.

It is quite possible that this conclusion was arrived at solely on what a person heard and saw. More likely, some of this conclusion came from subjective interpretations of past encounters. For example, if a man had a fight with his wife that morning he may be less patient than normal. He may have also unrealistically expected that his adversary would be more receptive to certain of his demands than he was.

In negotiations both sides are responding to the external stimulus of the other. To varying degrees they are also responding to unique inner stimuli: Does my opponent like me? Will my boss be satisfied with my presentations? I can tell this person is a jerk just by the way he looks at me. These internal stimuli can magnify or minimize our reaction to objective evidence that is crucial to wise decision-making.

The enclosed divorce mediation session illustrates how illogical inner reactions initially contaminated the visitation issue. The mother initially came to the conclusion that the father was selfish in his visitation demands.

Her conclusions may have been based on her own experience with her husband during the marriage. Her *expectation* was that he would continue to behave in that way in the future, not to her but to the children.

Now, if she had honestly examined the current evidence of his functioning and lifestyle she may not have come to the conclusion that he was still selfish. But to do so she would have to analyze her own assumptions and expectations of him: Was she expecting too much from him? Did she want to rupture his relationship with the children? Did she harbor immature wishful thinking that she had to protect her children from a bad father (husband)?

Conversely, these same subjective interpretations affected the father's judgment. Viewing his former wife as overprotective or even punitive, he proceeded to act in a way that would justify those beliefs. The same illogical mental rules applied to him; his expectation or even wish that his wife was out to get him allowed him to justify his anger. In a sense he was denying a possible reality that his wife respected his rights but truly believed she had to protect her children.

In order for people to make their wisest choices in negotiations, they must base them on objective and measurable criteria. In other words measure their reactions by what they see and hear. Each must conduct an honest assessment of their own expectations and measure whether they are reasonable. Perhaps they are anticipating their adversary to react in a certain unrealistic manner. We may be asking too much or too little from them. Also be aware that our own generalizations or stereotypes can create myopic views. Our adversaries, like ourselves, have rich inner lives that have a mixture of both good and bad traits. Good negotiators have to massage those positive traits to reach a good consensus.

Similar to putting a new frame around an old painting, conflictual reframing involves putting new words around harmful comments between disputants.

Well hidden in the harmful invectives uttered by one former spouse against the other, were legitimate issues that fueled such passionate attacks. Each one loved the children and could not tolerate irresponsible behavior on the other's part. Often the reason why these legitimate issues are not addressed properly is the manner in which they are presented. All of us have had the experience of someone addressing us with such words as "You didn't…" "You can't…" "You should…"

Our hair-raising resistance to learning the rest of that comment is almost assured.

Reframing is a conflict resolution skill designed to side step these self-protective instincts. It tweaks comments so that the gist or central message of remarks is accentuated. For example, in the narrative the former wife says to the former husband, "Look, you are not going to take your bimbo on visits with the children." However, justified or whatever brief satisfaction she derives from uttering this disrespectful comment, her pleasure is temporary. Her comment succeeds in removing any chance the couple has to make the best decision for their children. Ironically, the anger inherent in her comment stems from her desire to have a better and wiser visitation solution for her youngsters.

Consider if she had reassessed what her true objections were before uttering those words. However she may detest her former spouse, if she had said things his way she might guarantee the emotional health of her children. "I'm concerned for the children. They seem to be uncomfortable in the presence of your girlfriend. I know we love the children, can we talk about it?" However naïve some might believe this approach sounds in real life terms, it does work. People are more receptive to better options when they are swept along in the problem solving process.

As can be seen in this example, reframing normally consists of these three elements:

- It expresses your feelings ("I'm concerned, frustrated, angry," etc.)
- It describes the problem ("The presence of your girlfriend...")
- It communicates why a good solution is needed ("We love the children.")

REDEFINE THE CONFLICT

Kathy, a trained high-school peer mediator, has been asked by the school to intervene in a dispute between two female classmates. These students, both high school seniors have been involved in a series of arguments that purportedly involve a male classmate.

Kathy

(Mediator): Clara and Betty, you both know that I am a peer mediator at this school. I have been trained to help classmates who are involved in all different types of disputes, and I have successfully done this on many occasions. What I do is listen to each of you and help you to come up with different solutions to your problems. While you both probably believe that you have done nothing wrong, your misunderstanding has brought you to the attention of the principal and has not helped either of your reputations. I know that you were once friends, so let me help you work out your differences in a better way, okay?

This session is confidential. No one else will learn what is said here, including the principal. This process is voluntary. I cannot make you stay here. I hope that by what occurs here you will want to stay, but I cannot make you participate. I may want to speak to each of you separately to get some more information, and we may meet more than once. I will not make this decision for you—that is your job. My job is to ease your communication with one another and to help you look at your differences in another way. If we do resolve this problem you will be asked to help design an agreement that outlines your solution to the problem. Let's proceed.

Clara, can you tell me how these problems with Betty developed from your perspective?

Clara: Betty is an idiot! She has told everyone in this school that I stole her boyfriend. I wouldn't want that loser anyway!

Betty: A loser, ha! You can't even get a boyfriend. That's why you have to steal mine.

Mediator: Please, both of you stop. I'm sure if either of you were sitting in this chair you would see how immature you both sound. Obviously there is a lot of hurt—

Betty: (Interrupting) Clara is the biggest loser in the school. I want nothing to do with her. (Betty bolts from the session, while Clara remains.)

(Kathy decides to continue with a one-on-one session with Clara, hoping to engage Betty in a similar session later on.)

Mediator: I'm sorry the meeting started like this, Clara. Let's try again. What has happened between you and Betty?

Clara: (Tearfully) I wish that I knew. Betty and I have known each other since the second grade. She was one of my best friends. Last year we had even talked about going to the same college. About a month ago she became very cold to me. When I asked her if anything was wrong she wouldn't answer me. Later some of her friends said that I tried to "steal" her boyfriend. Apparently she was seeing this boy, Chuck, who asked me for some help with his homework one day at the library.

Mediator: I see. So this is all a mystery to you. Anything else that you think might be upsetting Betty?

Clara: Well, I don't know, but Betty has been hanging around with a different group of friends lately—sort of the fast crowd who we really didn't socialize with before. Betty was always worried about where she would go to college but now she says that she may not even go to college. It's like I don't know her anymore.

Mediator: So you're seeing a lot of personal changes in your friend too? Thanks for sharing that, Clara. I'm going to talk alone with Betty. Are you willing to meet together after that?

Clara: Yes.

Mediator: Good. (Kathy conducts a meeting alone with Betty the next day.)

Mediator: Want to tell me why you're so mad at Clara, Betty?

Betty: Clara always comes across as this perfect person. She had to decide what college we should apply to. The last straw was when she started to come on to this boy Chuck, who she knows I have liked since I saw him our freshman year. I also think she's mad because I've found some new friends.

Mediator: So I hear you saying several things, Betty. You resented the way Clara controlled things, and that may explain why you made some new friends. I also hear that you feel betrayed that she came on to Chuck, whom she knows you have liked for a long time. Is this right?

Betty: Yeah.

Mediator: I see. Well, that helps me. Anything else that I should know? (Betty shakes her head.)

Mediator: No? Would you be willing to meet with Clara again to see if we can get some answers to these issues?

Betty: I guess so. (Kathy conducts another mediation session with both parties.)

Mediator: As you both know, I have spoken to each of you about your views of the situation. Because you were such good friends, I believe that there is more than the usual amount of hurt and anger than I normally see in these mediations. However, the fact that you were such good companions tells me that you saw good qualities in one another that sustained that friendship. Maybe that friendship has changed, but let me see if I can help understand why it did. Clara, do you want to begin by discussing the incident with Chuck at the library?

Clara: Betty thinks that I am trying to take Chuck from her, but everyone knows that he talks to everyone at the library. He was asking me questions about her and wanted to know why we don't see each other as much anymore.

Betty: You're lying! You're just jealous!

Clara: I never even told you this before, Betty, but Chuck asked me out many times our sophomore year. I would never even consider it because I knew how much you liked him.

Betty: (Crying) You think you're so perfect.

Mediator: I don't hear Clara saying that, Betty. In fact I hear her saying how much she cares for you.

Clara: I don't understand how you could talk about me to everyone at school, Betty. I would never do that to you.

Betty: Everyone was laughing at me. I guess I don't know what to believe anymore. I'm sorry I said those things about you.

Clara: I'm sorry that we are not as close anymore. I didn't even know you were so angry with me for those other things. I guess we have both disappointed each other.

Betty: Yeah.

Mediator: It sounds to me like you both have been experiencing a lot of changes lately and both made wrong assessments about this situation with Chuck. Let's look at how your friendship can adapt to these changes without putting more stress in your lives, okay?

Clara and Betty: Yeah.

(1.) Conflicting parties often have shared issues and interests that must be identified and massaged properly.

Lost amid the misunderstandings, or worse, violence that attach to many conflicts are common threads that unite them. People often have to be helped to see these shared goals despite their frequent attempts not to see them. For example, Betty and Clara shared a common concern about their reputations in the school as well as a need not to get in trouble with school officials. Each was also united by their distinct fears: concerns about the future of their friendship as well as the future direction of their young lives. Each shared a sense of disappointment in the other. The friends' conflict also had a more existential common thread-each was developing her identity as maturing young adults who inevitably will make some poor choices as part of the maturation process.

These tangible and symbolic issues were not readily apparent early in the meeting between Betty and Clara. Their rather nasty insults of one another illustrates how quickly people opt for poor responses. If energy is directed at defending bruised egos, little energy is left for creative problem solving. In this conflict it took the labors of a resourceful mediator to identify the positive feelings that the two friends still had for one another.

In any conflict parties can uncover something that they have in common with one another. Those reinforced similarities can be the hidden motivators that encourage people to view a problem differently. It may be a simple reminder to both employers and employees that the resolution of a sexual harassment dispute may well decide if they will continue to have jobs within that troubled business. Similarly two tired fender bender antagonists do not normally want to end up in a hospital emergency room. A more positive resolution requires one clear-headed party to remind his tired adversary that neither party wants that to happen nor do they want to be involved in a costly lawsuit. That wise driver realizes that the poor release of that angry adrenaline can come at great expense. Such mature egos realize that one's sense of self does not have to be artificially reinforced by displays of aggressiveness.

Similar to this peer mediation case shared interests are often obscured within the party's antipathy for one another. To awaken these common treads that people share with one another takes careful listening and ingenuity. Clara and Betty's fears were not readily apparent. The mediator had to first earn each one's trust in order for each to reveal her vulnerabilities. The future of their friendship rested on their ability to see how their own failures had contributed to their growing misunderstanding. In addition the mediator gently reminded them that their reputations were both being damaged by their ongoing spat.

Often even when these shared interests are obvious people choose to overlook them. This fact demonstrates how strong is the need to protect one's ego from presumed harm. For example, in the divorce narrative in Chapter 7, the parents had an obvious shared need to ensure that their children emerged form this divorce as healthy as possible. They then went about assaulting one another in a way that would almost guarantee trauma for the children.

It takes the resources of a talented mediator or even one parent to defuse this type of blame and concentrate on their shared mission. The goal–in this case to work together for the betterment of the children— must be constantly kept in focus. Often the mediator or negotiator models the very type of behavior that they want to see in the other side. If that person refrains from responding to personal attacks and models respect, a respectful atmosphere is created. Only that type of atmosphere would help less defensive parents to focus on the welfare of their children.

Most conflicts have many shared interests—some blatant and others well hidden. All or only one may be the impetus to help parties be more cooperative with one another. Identifying which have the most relevance to the participants is very important. For example, in the group home mediation in the previous chapter the altruistic spirit that both sides brought to the table—to help the disadvantaged in a special way—may have been the deciding factor in licensing the facility.

Often the parties have to be helped to see shared interests that they may not wish to see. A labor negotiator about to begin what he views as hard negotiations with management may well be focused on his representative's needs. He often has to be stimulated to appreciate the needs of management. Why? His would not be the first company that spent its way out of business with an overly generous benefit package. The shared interest—the economic health of the company—was not a proper focus of the negotiations.

(2.) A person's view of the conflict must be shaped by images that it is in his best interest to resolve it in a healthy fashion.

In most conflicts the answer to this internal question decides how people will act in resolving it: How is my action or decision going to benefit me? The job of the other side is to find their adversary's answer to that question. Often the failure to even consider that question never mind attempt to answer it is the reason for the conflicts escalation. For opponents often make assumptions about the other side's needs that have little reflection on the other party's motivation. Many people believe that other people are always motivated by some tangible award such as money, land or rent when in fact people are often looking for more symbolic rewards such as power, control or love. Throughout this text we have seen the need for angry mothers, frustrated students and abused women to be validated and recognized in a certain way. That validation often was more important than having cleaner dishes, better grades or safer homes.

The job of any conflict solver is to assess how people uniquely interpret those benefits. For example we have seen how insecure people can be manipulated if opponents recognize that they act to prove something about themselves. Thus someone could be co-opted to act a certain way to prove how smart, competent or nice they are. For example, a deserving employee may not challenge her employer's refusal to give her a pay raise. Although angry, she decides not to readdress the issue because it would force her to challenge her identity as a nice person. A salesperson may convince a timid buyer with the words, "It would be a smart purchase." Only the customer insecure about his own competencies would be swayed by such words. Such people can also be extremely frustrating in bargaining situations. Their decision-making is not based on external factors associated with solving the problem but on satisfaction of these internal needs. Thus someone may not accept a reasonable offer of settlement because he is fearful of looking weak, incompetent or whatever personal need motivates them. In the above peer mediation case, one friend had a need to seek out new friends and experiences. That independence also came with a knowledge that she may not be able to trust these new friends. Her friend Clara may have symbolized all of the ambivalence that she felt—safety versus change. The mediation process helped Betty to realize that these changes may have been the true sources of her anger.

Often adversaries are seeking benefits that are illusionary in nature. A community may object to a group home until they realize that the next-in line tenant plans to open an adult store on the site. The Middle East situation also represents this concept of people striving for false benefits. People die daily over specially conceived land that is considered far more important to the majority of its citizens than safe homes, good jobs and education of the young. The same earth that is soiled with their blood could be toiled to provide food for all. The difficult job is to help people to see that destroying their enemy may not result in better futures for their young members. One day those mental images may help to foster long term peace between these combatants.

Often the satisfaction of immediate needs may have unhealthy long-term benefits. For example, a country ruled by a despot may immediately squelch any internal dissent by violent means. Diplomatic intervention may help its leaders to realize that their world image and less foreign aid may be the cost of any shortsighted responses. Obviously this proves that benefit reexamination does not have to have an altruistic basis to be effective.

This type of benefit analysis helps us to understand how people become more cooperative with one another. If people receive pleasure from their communications with us, are respectfully listened to, complimented or asked to express their ideas more fully—they become more compliant. Their gain is the recognition they feel better about themselves as a result of the positive relations. Conversely poor relationships are marred by aloof and defensive communications. The parties are prepared to receive little benefit from the relationship when suspicious of the intent of the other.

(3.) These images must demonstrate that a change in their thinking will result in a gain and not a loss.

Often it is the manner in which a disputant views a problem that determines how it will be resolved. For example, if one country views making a concession on a boundary issue as a sign of weakness it will probably not surrender this land without a fight. If the same issue is looked upon as affording a gain—a gain in security or safety—they may well look at the forfeiture of land differently. It is that attitude in which a dispute is assessed that often determines how it is resolved. Those negotiators who can explore a dispute from all angles—who creatively dissect how solutions can meet people's needs in a positive way have the most success.

People do not like losses. They are perceived in a negative way and, consciously or unconsciously, are avoided as signs of pain, shame or weakness. Normally a person will fight harder to avoid rather than to obtain a gain. In poor economic times labor is more apt to relent on a salary increase next year rather than give up benefits it already has. In the landlord tenant dispute in Chapter 4 the landlord was initially prepared to litigate his tenant's eviction no matter the cost. His fight, the result of the feeling that his tenant was winning their battle, would result in the exact opposite goal that he wanted—to get his son in the apartment as soon as possible.

This fact also explains why people will continue to invest in losses even when they realize the situation is hopeless. A divorced father may continue to rack up unaffordable legal fees to acquire custody of children who won't even see him. To give up this fight may require him to confront aspects of himself that he may not like. In other words this type of self-revealing loss is more painful than giving up on the issue. He may rationalize his behavior as a need to protect or help his children but he fails to question how his relationship has reached such a poor status.

Creative problem solvers help parties to see that a particular resolution results in a gain for them and not a loss. The non-custodial father may be helped to see that his children may wish to see him if he removes the pressure of a custody suit. Thus his relationship with the children and their mental health may actually improve by dropping his petition. In the sexual harassment case in Chapter 6, management resisted giving in to the harassed female employees. They probably feared that they would be taken advantage of if they relented to the women. Management had to be convinced that they were making positive choices to improve the company culture. Such movement on their part would result in happier, more productive employees. Thus the same facts in a dispute can be manipulated in a manner that consensus is perceived as a win in some way rather than a loss. Clara and Betty's dispute was layered with similar feelings of loss. Each felt betrayed by the other while also realizing that dramatic changes awaited each of them in the next year. The peer mediator portrayed the dispute in a more positive way—that their friendship was still a strong one and could endure albeit in a different way than previously.

Such an attitude shift is not easy. People often resist absorption of these benefits even when they make sense. Such people often feel victimized by the other side and the consequent lack of trust in that person raises mental defenses to defeat new approaches. The divorced father considering the dropping of the custody suit may blame his spouse for his conflicts with the children. In a flash, those dark images supercede any positive outcomes that he can consider.

To attain these goals people have to become comfortable with a new way of thinking. The beauty of structured negotiations, such as ROCCO Four Rs, is that it is designed for people to become internally comfortable with a new way of thinking. As people talk, assess and even resist certain approaches, they also become more comfortable with viewing the conflict differently. Often they have to justify their beliefs that do not fit in to the facts. For example, Betty came to the self-realization that the anger projected at Clara about the rift was unjustified. She had to absorb and internalize this information for herself however before she would come to accept it. As her ego became comfortable with this realization she became open to different solutions to the conflict.

(4.) Communications that lead to the most meaningful disclosures between adversaries invariably lead to the best agreements.

Our deepest and most intimate conversations with others result in exchanges of information with deep meaning. Life-long friends require little time to reveal their deepest fears, joys or problems with each other. Negotiations have little ability to reach this type of intimacy between opponents with different interests. But there is one similarity to communications with friends that are crucial to negotiations with strangers—the need for each to reveal their deepest needs with each other. This does not mean that they have to like each other, however to bargain successfully. Bargaining comfort refers to a style of communication in which parties identify with their similarities with one another: People who realize that the other side cares about their thoughts and has the ability to understand them. People who respectfully acknowledge their opponent's views even when they disagree with them. People who are astute enough to capture the hidden or deeper feelings associated with certain issues that have great significance to their adversary.

The ability to form a relationship with an adversary rests on the ability to engage in communications of some meaning between them. Shallow arguments between complex personalities with a variety of needs demonstrate the flammable potential of conflict when little is revealed between them. But with a little respectful prodding each may realize that their needs or reasons for acting a certain way make sense if seen from the other's perspective.

Often one side may not like what they see of the person they have come to know. But that knowledge of their adversary may help them to resolve a dispute. A dictator may not care what a diplomatic envoy thinks of his brutal repression of his people. He may care about his world image or legacy as a world leader and reconsider policies that affect that view. The ability to acquire that information from him was based on the envoys substantive communication style.

Reflection of meaning responses are designed to get to those deeper layers of communication that build understanding and trust. In them one side gives accurate feedback of the other's comments. That reflection, however, includes both the content and emotion behind the communication.

It captures the why of a particular issue—the deepest significance of the sender's message. Betty and Clara's recognition that their friendship was important to them at the end of their session was preceded by a series of messages that had deep meaning to each of them. Each revealed their fear and vulnerabilities which laid just beneath the surface of their anger.

Let's demonstrate a technical reflection of meaning statement that builds cooperation. A divorce mediator may hear the following statement from a divorced mom speaking about the father, "I can't stand it when he constantly brings the children home late from visits. He makes his own rules just like he did when we were married." This woman has to hear that the deeper context to her message has been understood by someone. She needs it so that she can feel comfortable that the mediator is competent enough to understand the depth of her feelings plus that she will be prodded to share more of herself with the mediator. Thus the mediator might respond, "I see. Beyond your frustration that he doesn't respect your schedule with the children his tardiness reminds you of the control he exerted during the marriage." This statement hopefully leads to the deeper issue in the couple's relationship that needs exploring—whether she is right about this issue of control and powerlessness that permeated the marriage. For that hidden agenda is probably why they fight over every small issue involving the children.

The mediator's reflection of meaning response can be broken down into three components the mother had to hear: the Facts—"Bring the children home late," the Feelings—"I can't stand it," and her Reasoning—"Just like he did when we were married." Now, more comfortable that the mediator understood why she is so frustrated, her feelings about the issue can be further explored. In addition, the father hearing the same words in the session also better understands the meaning to her anger. She may not be someone trying to raise a ruckus over what he perceives as a small tardiness problem. Rather she may be dealing with the same aftermath feelings of loss from a divorce that all parents must address. Now, more comfortable that the mediator understood why she is so frustrated her feelings about the issue can be further explored. In addition, the father hearing the same words in the session also better understands the meaning behind her anger.

REASONED NOT REGRETFUL RESOLUTIONS

This is a dispute between a private business and a community group of concerned citizens. The business implements and staffs group homes in various cities and towns for emotionally disabled adults. A citizens group was formed as a result of community unease about the project. Litigation was commenced by this group seeking an injunction to stop the home. The court has referred the two sides to mediation to see if a settlement can be reached. This is the first meeting of the parties.

Mediator: Please allow me to introduce myself. My name is Cynthia Martin. I am your court referred mediator.

    In my experience the judge would not have referred this matter to mediation unless he thought it would benefit you in some way. In that spirit I simply ask you to keep your mind open to the possibility that we will make the wisest decision possible. My job is to help you acquire the most accurate information on the issues surrounding this proposal and to create an atmosphere where people want to make the best decision. In that vein I ask each of you to be patient with me as I acquire this information and please don't interrupt one another. I will listen to each of you equally. One suggestion I do have is that when you speak discuss how these issues impact you. In other words don't blame the other side for your feelings—help the other side to understand them. Okay?

    Before we begin I would like to share some ground rules about mediation. This process is confidential. Nothing we say here can be used in court. I cannot testify as to my feelings, nor will have to share details of any proposals made here. This process is voluntary. I cannot make you stay here and each side is free to pursue litigation. I must remain impartial—my only goal is to foster the proper problem solving climate that allows you to reach an agreement. If we do reach an agreement, I will help to draft it and present it to the Court. Are there any questions about my role or the process of mediation? No, good. Let's begin. Mr. Smith, would you like to share your concerns?

Mr. Smith: (He is the representative of the community coalition against the home.) I'm sick of these people coming in to our community. What are we, a dumping ground for society's problems? Why don't you put the home in your town, Mr. Jacobs?

Mr. Jacobs: (He is the representative of the private for-profit group home company.) We have homes in all types of socio-economic areas, Mr. Smith. This site fits for a number of reasons...

Mr. Smith: (interrupting) Are you kidding me? We get crackpots and they get golf courses. Why don't you move next door to the home Jacobs?

Mediator: (to Mr. Smith) Please, let me understand this proposal better. (turning to Mr. Jacobs) How is this site beneficial to the community?

Mr. Jacobs: Well, most of the residents will come from this community. The area is close to many of their jobs and is accessible to public transportation.

Mediator: So you're stating that the residents will represent this community and that this location will meet their vocational and transportation needs?

Mr. Jacobs: Yes, we'll also spend money...

Mr. Smith: (interrupting again) We don't want these nuts around our kids. It's as simple as that. (Turning to Mediator) Do you have children? Would you want to live in this type of fear?

Mediator: I can certainly understand your feelings, Mr. Smith. Please try to consider that your fears may be allowing you to justify your angry demeanor which is not helping us right now, okay? (to Mr. Jacobs) Can you understand these concerns, Mr. Jacobs?

Mr. Jacobs: Of course I do. I have children, so I would also have concerns. Our company has homes throughout the country. We pride ourselves on working closely with each community and respond quickly to any problems with residents. We have never had any violence with these residents, who are carefully screened.

Mr. Smith: Like I'm supposed to believe you. Our property values go down while your profits go up.

Mr. Jacobs: I'm getting sick of these insinuations, Mr. Smith. If you want to settle this in court I am confident that we will be successful.

Mr. Smith: If that's a threat you'd better be careful. Those windows in your home may have a series of bad accidents.

Mediator: Look folks, you both know that you are free to pursue your relief in court at any time. The stakes are high, however, and please consider the cost of throwing up your hands in resignation: perhaps expensive litigation, bad publicity for the town and most importantly loss of a potential good home for its most vulnerable residents. I don't know yet Mr. Smith if your assumptions about this home have been adequately tested. Your fears may ultimately be proven correct, but they may also be false. My job is to help you make the most informed decision based on facts and not on assumptions. Do you know how we can help solve this dilemma Mr. Jacobs?

Mr. Jacobs: I'll be happy to provide the community with all our safety records and allow them to tour one of our homes. Contrary to popular belief, property values have risen in communities that we have homes. We spend money proactively in the community and contribute to the tax-base.

Mediator: Can you give an example of this proactive community approach?

Mr. Jacobs: Sure. We spend money upgrading playgrounds and hosting recreation days. Many of the residents of our home are involved in these activities, serving as judges or speaking to schools about mental illness.

Mediator: If these issues turn out to be true Mr. Smith, would that alter your views about the home?

Mr. Smith: I guess our committee could look at one of these homes. I just don't want anyone taking advantage of us. There may be some things about these homes that we have not considered before…

(1.) A person's reaction to his differences with others often prevents him from choosing the best solutions to that conflict.

This writer has seen countless negotiations fail because adversaries adopt conclusions that they wish to see. Often their poor solutions reflect more on their reactions or expectations than on the merits of the dispute. The above narrative hopefully illustrates this problem. The mediator could not even get the community representative to consider any possible benefits of the home until those fears were carefully examined.

If we analyze this dispute the true issue under scrutiny is: What was the best solution for this community in terms of having such a home in their midst? Included in this definition is a concern for the proposed residents of the facility. If the company was right, there might be a net gain to the community in terms of increased tax benefits and related town improvements. Moreover, there may be personal value in helping their fellow neighbors who have special needs and possibly special talents to give to it. On the other hand, the company may be wrong in their site conclusions, and a better location may suit everyone's needs. Of course the company may be embellishing their information, or worse, lying about it. This is an operational problem that exists in any negotiation-one side wishing to fulfill their own needs any way they can. The problem in this negotiation was that, at least initially, these issues could not even be tested.

Ideally, in any negotiation the participants proceed like two collaborators trying to solve a complex problem. At the end of the day when all the facts have been carefully scrutinized the sides may still be in disagreement. But the focus would have remained on the problem and not on the people. When decisions are made on evidence and not expectations the wisest solutions result.

Like many disputes, however [the Middle East comes quickly to mind] the group home dispute did not focus on the problem. Why not? The answer is as simple as it is complex. A person's gaze at his opposition is often tarnished by his own unusual perceptions. The community representative's expectation that "crackpots" would endanger his town included a handful of untested fears. Furthermore his belief that the wealthy company was "dumping" its problem on them further fueled his unhealthy cynicism. Without testing these concerns, Mr. Smith acted on them as if these were facts. Bolstered by this assumption-turned-fact logic, Mr. Smith could easily justify his own aggressive tactics as being reasonable.

He was also guilty of characterizing the dispute in broad generalizations. Man's mind is a tidy one and it is often easy to label someone as "uncaring or untrustworthy" and act on these generalizations, rather than to absorb all of the nuances associated with resolving a complex problem. This occurs for several reasons. Human thinking often evolves in an economical pattern that looks to a single cause for a problem. The recent Boston Red Sox failure to bring a coveted World Series win to their fans was considered the direct result of the mangers' poor decision-making. That simple logic did not require those same fans to consider the many earlier opportunities the team had, to put the game away. In a similar way, Mr. Smith's firm mindset had a luxury in that he did not have to consider the complexities associated with solving this issue.

It is also easy to attribute bad motives to someone who holds opinions different than our own. Mr. Smith easily concluded that company profits were the sole motivation for the proposed home because it fit neatly into his simple beliefs. His position had the added psychological benefit that he did not have to appear indecisive, which can provoke anxiety, or worse make the wrong decision about the home.

Rocco's 4R's offers a model for people to maintain the same comfort level in their decision-making, but discreetly challenges them to test their stereotypes. It creates a need in their minds that conflict requires an objective analysis to reach the wisest solutions that human minds can muster.

This stimulation process begins with recognition that good solutions often lie within these brittle generalities. As long as the citizen group hides behind stereotypes that "crackpots" will damage their communities no reasonable discourse is possible. Discussion must center on specifics: How many residents will there be at the home? What is their diagnosis? How many violent incidents have occurred in their homes? What type of security is provided to the community? What are the potential benefits to the community?

A special communications process can penetrate these untested beliefs. To persuade someone to consider another's viewpoints one must get them to think seriously about them. Getting in the way is their own comfortable thinking. To talk in specifics about your ideas requires mental focus even if it is simply to oppose you. As the parties share more and more information about the "crackpots"—even to muster up support for their own arguments— they have to justify their arguments with logic. A dialogue emerges that is not based on fears or emotional reactions but on their true differences.

Normally after a fact-finding atmosphere has been created the party with the stronger facts can almost self-persuade an opponent to see the logic of certain solutions. Any adversary is always careful to have their opponent receive some gain from the resolution however. One-sided agreements are rarely successful; people can resist them in many clever ways from outright legal resistance to a work slow down. That gain may have symbolic value that is as important as tangible gain. For example, Mr. Smith may feel compelled to resist the home because of public pressure even when convinced the home can have advantages to the community. A resolution that provides a three year lease for the home with a citizen's advisory board headed by Mr. Smith could be a hypothetical proposal that is aired. Like a window shade lighting a darkened room, the parties' stimulus to consider wiser proposals results in brighter results for all parties.

(2.) Reasoned conflict resolution uses objective and not emotional evidence to resolve disputes.

Aroused that someone opposes them people can easily misconstrue the intent of another's remarks. Misunderstandings breed from reactions rather than understanding. While some of these reactions are prepared ones—Mr. Smith's preconceived biases against the group home—others result from the words or actions of their opponent. Ironically some of these differences are more illusionary than real. How often do we hear people claim that they will respond to another in the way that they are treated? When conflict occurs these messages are often confusing and each side may be reacting to behaviors that neither side intends. Instead each side is responding to false messages that quickly cascade to greater and greater misunderstanding. Soon each side's message is a reaction to the other's message and the true disputes lay unaddressed.

For example in the above mediation Mr. Jacobs eventually tires of Mr. Smith's charges and threatens that the Court will have to handle the dispute. Although Mr. Jacobs probably recognized that the best resolution involved the input of the community members, his frustration—his emotional response—interfered with further patient problem solving. His response may have been different if he realized that fear prompted Mr. Smith's angry demeanor. His response could then be directed at easing those fears rather than responding to the anger.

Rocco's Four Rs creates a special problem solving forum that airs the full dimension of behavior in conflict. Rather than focus on one word or action of either side it allows for the full disclosure of their opponent's needs and wishes. In that full dimension study of their adversary lie needs that can spur parties to act differently. For instance let us suppose that this community does pride itself on lending a hand to a troubled neighbor. In other words, they have altruistic motivations that are being obscured in their initial opposition to the home. If the business credibly mixes making a profit with caring for the residents, then they share a common ground with one another. That mutual thread may be the foundation that will lead to greater trust for one another.

One of the dangers in conflict is that our use of language has different meaning to each of us depending on our past experiences. A person who has been abused as a child will certainly have a different reaction to the word child abuse than someone who has not. Similarly one company may find as unreasonable the strong resistance from a community group to a home that another company has determined as reasonable and consequently prepared to defend with persuasive evidence.

The other difficulty with language is that people respond to words as if they always reflect reality. For example, Mr. Smith initially used the adjective "crackpots" to describe the residents of the home.

Besides its inflammatory nature, the term did not adequately reflect the array of mental illness that exists. Were there to be residents with minor anxiety attacks? Were some of the people suffering from simple depression? Would residents have more severe illnesses such as dementia, psychosis or manic disorders?

Throughout this text we have seen evidence of people quickly labeling someone as "unfair," "cheap" or "controlling" and acting on these images as if they reflected reality. What they are responding to is their own reaction to the person which may or may not reflect whether they are right. What has to be tested is the evidence that supports these conclusions.

In the divorce mediation in Chapter 7, we vividly see how one's descriptions can adversely impact on conflict. The mother describes how her children will "hate" their father for his selfish behavior. He angrily responds that she will selfishly make sure that this outcome occurs. In other words that she will control the children's feelings about him. Both of those conclusions have to be further tested with facts by the mediator. The mother would have to give examples when the father was selfish with the children. How often did those incidents occur? What was the most recent example of this type of behavior? The father would also be similarly asked to quantify his views: What incidents convince you that the mother is controlling? How often did they occur, etc? Each parent would also have to reconcile examples when the other parent displayed behavior that disconfirmed their conclusions, i.e., the mother allowing the father unscheduled visits with the children; the father giving up visits for the mother's birthday.

What this process does is replace untested reactions with facts. For facts are the nuggets that drive wise conflict resolutions. Words in and of themselves have no measurable value. Finding out how much, how often, and what price, gives a quantifiable aspect to statements. In the exchange that uncovers these facts the parties are using rational arguments to resolve their dispute rather than untested reactions.

(3.) Preparation away from the bargaining table is as important as action at the bargaining table.

A common failure among many negotiators is that they bargain in a one-sided manner. Comfortable with the soundness of their own positions, adversaries often pound away at each other trying to convince the other side to adopt their views. Each side is often stunned with their opponent won't accept their "can't miss" logic.

Their failure is attributable to the fact that they have analyzed only one-half of the problem. For after acquiring all of the facts that support their position; developing a bargaining strategy to achieve those goals; and assessing what they will do if an agreement is not reached they must answer those same questions for their opponent. When they do so, the strange or unreasonable positions of their adversaries often make more sense. By understanding your opponents viewpoints one learns that many solutions may exist to solve a problem rather than just one solution.

If Mr. Jacobs, the representative of the group home business had done that type of homework the session may not have become as volatile. For example, he may have invited community members from other towns where the homes are located to address the group. They may have eased safety concerns and addressed some positive qualities these residents have made to their town. The town's altruistic spirit may have naturally stimulated more interest in the project.

Perhaps a true story which occurred nearly one hundred years ago demonstrates our need to understand our opponent. Toward the conclusion of the Presidential elections of 1912, Theodore Roosevelt planned a final whistle stop tour through Middle America. His supporters, seeking a final advantage in this closely fought election, had arranged for the publication of three million pamphlets with Roosevelt's picture on them. They were to be distributed to the public at every train stop.

Just prior to the tour a campaign worker noticed the the photograph had a copyright insignia which read "C" Moffet Studio, Chicago Illinois. The unauthorized use of the photograph could cost up to $1.00 per photo. Campaign workers despaired due to both the excessive copyright cost, plus the fact that the tour was to begin within several days.

From the campaign's perspective the situation was hopeless. If they alerted the studio to the dilemma they had little leverage to negotiate a fair price. If they said nothing they risked up to three million dollars in damages as well as bad publicity. If they did not distribute the pamphlets, they could well lose the election.

One of the campaign managers contacted a noted financier and Roosevelt supporter, George Perkins for advice. Perkins immediately summoned a stenographer and dispatched the following cable to Moffet Studios: *"We are planning to distribute many pamphlets with Roosevelt's picture on the cover. It will be great publicity for the studio whose photograph that we use. How much will you pay us to use yours? Respond immediately."* Shortly after he received this reply, *"We have never done this before, but under the circumstances we would be pleased to offer $250."* It is believed that Perkins accepted this price without making a counteroffer![1].

Without assessing how his opponent saw the same facts that he did, Perkins would not have been able to develop such a simple strategy. Perkins's genius is that he considered the needs of the studio. He quickly realized that Moffet would not even be aware of the stress that confronted their side. He

---

[1]   Lax, David and Sebenius, James K. The Manager as Negotiator, New York Free Press, 1966

carefully crafted a proposal that promised financial gain to the studio but little time for them to consider why Perkins was making this offer.

Good negotiators also study the objective tendencies of their adversaries. How trustworthy are they? What has been their history of negotiations? Have the negotiations been marred by litigation or threats? Who will represent the other side? What is his or her bargaining style?

An old adage states that a battle is often won before it begins. Mr. Smith could have prepared his homework on the company even before the first meeting with it. He could have utilized newspaper articles, trade journals, and state licensing reports, to name only a few resources to learn about the company's reputation. He could also have learned what the company's options were in the communities they were rebuffed in.

Rocco's Four Rs examines conflict as if it were basting over a slow-burning rotisserie. The problem must be assessed from all angles: yours, theirs, professional appraisers, teachers, and campaign managers. The wisest solution often emerges through the smoke-filled haze which too often blinds combative adversaries.

(4.) Motivational Bargaining involves specialized methods to help your opponent to see your way of thinking.

To bargainer's constant amazement, our adversaries often cling to their positions with pit-bull like tenacity. Their persistent cling often survives irrefutable evidence that their position does not make sense or that wiser options are available. Throughout this text we have seen how angry landlords, obstinate employers and insensitive parents behaved in ways that they probably realized only exacerbated the conflict. It is obvious that the need which motivates this behavior is not always a logical one. Our beliefs are precious to us; while some serve to make wise decisions others serve to relieve temporary tensions that overwhelm us. This part of the chapter is devoted to this second type of decision-making. How do we motivate people to alter their beliefs? Even better, how do we persuade them to accept our beliefs?

Seasoned negotiators quickly have to learn that people like control over their decision-making. Bullying tactics simply do not work. Even if one side wears down the other and an agreement is hatched, the terms are rarely fulfilled. The resentment by the "defeated" party, often at their disappointment at themselves, will spoil any victory felt by the conqueror.

Of course, control implies that choices or alternatives are available for them to resolve a dispute. One of the initial dilemmas in the group home conflict was to convince the community advocate that he had many opportunities to control decisions about this home. Rather than viewing this as a dangerous object being dropped into their midst, the community had many choices to consider: How many residents would be at the home? What are their diagnoses? What could they offer to the community as benefits? What were the alternative sites for the home?

The mediator helped this process in a number of ways. First, she outlined the options and alternatives that existed to reduce the community's fears. Since the parties could choose to develop their own strategies they were less likely to resist options being "sold" to them from a third party. Their preferences enhance their perception of personal control which normally results in better compliance with agreements. Lastly, the mediator expressed optimism that the parties were capable of carrying out these plans. This encouragement further stimulated the participants that not only could they choose their own solutions, but that they were capable of carrying them out.

A related motivational tool is in the formulation of participants' goals. One should be asked to define what he hopes to get out of the particular negotiation or mediation. Rather than someone else diagnosing their perception of the problem, parties must be helped to define their own awareness of what separates the disputants. Once those goals have been defined, the parties are then asked to compare those goals to the current state of affairs. Their own recognition of where they currently are in the dispute and where they hope to be, serves as a motivation to consider better alternatives. For example, in Chapter 6, a business was accused of having a work environment that was insensitive to female employees. In rejecting those opinions, the company outlines their views as to what type of company culture that they desired. The owners were then asked to consider what had motivated several employees to make similar claims of impropriety against it. In other words, the company had to justify why such a good company culture could have several female employees threatening lawsuits. This image seemed to prompt the participants to consider new company policies.

Similarly in Chapter 4, a frustrated landlord's sole motivation was to get his tenant out of the unit as soon as possible. The mediation process allowed him to see that his angry behavior was only making his tenant more resolute that she would remain there. By focusing on his long term goal—to get his son into the apartment—he was stimulated to solve the problem differently. Ironically, he even helped the tenant to get subsidized housing.

The last motivational tactic is a stimulus in the negative sense. Parties often have to be vividly reminded of the negative consequences of continued conflict. Parties have to be reminded as to the costs of continued conflict. In the community home case, both sides might become mired in litigation for years. The town's reputation may be smeared unfairly and the potential residents may have lost an opportunity to be part of a great community. The trick is to use those factors that have the most relevance to the participants. A selfish college professor may not be sensitive to his student's private issues, but he may readjust his attitude if he thought his reputation among his peers would be sullied.

ROCCO'S TEN COMMANDMENTS TO WISE CONFLICT RESOLUTION

1. Even good people possess an almost instinctual ability to exaggerate their differences with others. *Don't let the door hit you on the backside.*

2. What we "see"—our assumptions or perceptions about others— is the silent contributor to most conflicts. *I thought I told you to clean the dishes. You're just plain lazy!*

3. When perceived to be criticized, evaluated or resisted, our first instinct is to carelessly react, rather than deliberately respond to our opponent. *Don't give me one of your explanations.*

4. People fail to see that their own good intentions do not always translate into their own good behavior. *You're not going to amount to anything.*

5. Our adversaries may also misinterpret our intent from our words. *Ma, I have an explanation.*

6. Consequently, each party is blinded to the fact that the opposing party's negative behavior may be a reaction to his own behavior. *Maybe I'll just go live with dad.*

7. In due course each side justifies and minimizes his own role in the dispute and maximizes the worst inferences drawn from his opponent's behavior. *You're threatening me?*

8. An escalating cycle of misunderstanding flourishes as the parties increasingly respond to each other rather than to the true issues. *You will end up a loser, just like your father.*

9. Wise conflict resolution requires recognition that people's similarities with one another are greater than their differences. *I didn't want to bother you at work.*

10. Rocco's Four Rs quickly restructures these conflicted rhythms by establishing a wise-problem-solving momentum that replaces regret with reason. *You're the only thing that is important to me.*

PUTTING IT ALL TOGETHER

The following is a hypothetical model of an actual divorce mediation. (It will be herein referred to as divorce mediation, but the concepts will apply to many family disputes, such as paternity, child custody, and adoption cases.) The family law arena is one in which formal mediation has thrived in recent years. It joins many other commonly mediated disputes such as labor management, landlord/tenant, medical malpractice, and small-claims conflicts as areas of mediation growth. The participants in such conflicts recognize that mediated disputes are more emotionally satisfying, less expensive, and last longer.

In divorce mediations participants have to agree to certain conditions. Initially they must both agree to come to the bargaining table voluntarily. They must also adhere to the central tenants of mediation, such as honesty and respect for the process. They have to be transparent in all their financial issues. Should a hidden bank account or inheritance be revealed, the mediation is terminated, and such concealment may be revealed to a Court. The parties appear in mediation without attorneys, but they are encouraged to bring an agreement from a legal representative for review. While some mediators are specially trained lawyers, (many are also mental health professionals) these attorneys do not "represent" either side. Their role is to expertly guide the communications to help each side come to an agreement that satisfies his or her needs.

Family law mediation often proceeds in the following manner. Each participant submits a personal statement outlining the current situation and how he or she would want each issue to be resolved. Common issues that must be resolved are (1) custody and visitation with the children of the relationship, (2) the vacating or relocation of the marital home, and (3) how such disputes will be resolved in the future. The financial issues generally fall into these areas, (1) child support and alimony, (2) resolution of medical and insurance issues, and (3) division of assets, including homes and vehicles, inheritances (only acquired during marriage), pensions and retirement accounts, and other tangible assets, i.e. furniture, jewelry, heirlooms, etc.

In the ensuing divorce narrative the facts are as follows: Jack and Sue Smith are ages 50 and 49 respectively. They married shortly after Sue graduated from college, and have been married 25 years. They have three children; a daughter Julie, age 19, who is a freshman at a nearby college, a son Jack Jr., age 17, who is a junior in high school, and a daughter Mary, age 12, who is in the seventh grade. The couple separated ten months ago. Jack currently lives in a nearby city with his parents, while Sue remains in the marital home with the two younger children.

Jack works as a plumber in the family business started by his father. Early in the marriage Sue worked as an elementary school teacher. For the past several years, however, she has worked as a teacher's aide as the couple had agreed years earlier that this allowed her more time to raise the children.

Jack has an annual income of $100,000, which has been consistent for many years. Sue makes $20,000 as a teacher's aide. The couple own the marital home valued at approximately $450,000 with a mortgage of $125,000. They own a vacation cottage worth $150,000 and mortgage free, which was given to them by Jack's parents years ago. The couple owns two vehicles, which are debt free. Jack has a profit sharing plan in his plumbing business valued at $450,000 and bank accounts worth roughly $50,000. That is the extent of their assets.

Prior to this mediation the couple went to court. Jack was ordered to pay $600 per week child support in accordance with state child support guidelines. He sees the children every other weekend at his parents' home where he lives.

Each parent submitted a position statement with me prior to the first session. In it each parent outlined a "wish" list as to the outcome of the divorce mediation. I categorized these wishes into goals.

I will "Read the Conflict" as I review them and assess how realistic each side's positions are from these statements. As notably, I will question why these particular outcomes are important to each side. Do they reflect basic interests and needs to function in this new family structure? What deeper fears or anxieties may be reflected from these statements? What assumptions or prejudices seem to exist in either parent? How does either side view his role in the dispute? Does the couple seem emotionally mature? These issues and many more will have to be "Read" further in our meetings.

The first meeting is crucial in any mediation. I want to create trust in the process. I do not know at this point what type of interpersonal momentum I will encounter. I will have to be extremely conscious to Restructure the Interpersonal Momentum in the early stages of mediation. I must prepare for impediments to reasoned decision making early when trust in the process is lacking. In general, the more tenuous the communication process, *the more active are my interventions.* The stronger the cooperation of the participants, the more passive are my interventions. The core philosophy of neutrality and ultimate ownership of the problem solving on the parties is stressed in the first meetings. The participants are asked not to interrupt one another and write down comments if necessary while the other side has time to speak. I may do private sessions with each side prior to the joint session or call one if a session becomes turbulent. The husband and wife here would be asked to speak in a respectful way and refrain from vulgarities. In my own practice I ask participants to refrain as much as possible from using the pronoun "you," but advocate use of the pronoun "I." As I identified earlier in the text, "reframing" dramatically alters the reception of a remark. Rather than defending a position, "I" statements encourage understanding. In essence I am modeling the type of behavior I wish to create in both sides. My respect for the process and the problems often leads to a similar respect by the parties.

Our mediation will now begin. I have to be conscious to Restructure the Interpersonal Momentum at all times, but especially during the early stages of mediation. As any mediation unfolds I am constantly assessing how, when, and why certain information is revealed. I self-question. Is it relevant to the ultimate goals of this family? Should this information be addressed now or can it wait? I am also examining what is not being said, and ask myself why it isn't asked. Simultaneously, I am examining the communication style of each side. Are one or both sides overtly or passively attacking one another? What are the "hot spots" in the couple's relationship—subjects that chronically create tensions for them. What are the non-verbal clues revealing to me about each side—the frowns, sighs, or folding of arms?

(As the mediation unfolds I will use parentheses to add my thoughts on these subjects. Often there is no right or wrong intervention, and I may decide to intervene or not, solely on instinct. This is the "art" of mediation. Other mediators could use different approaches and get the same results for this family. My point is that the turbulence pushing the domestic waters can get the parties downstream by a number of different routes.)

Mediator (a general question to both parties): Perhaps we might begin with assessing how each of you sees your lives five years from now when Mary leaves for college.

Susan: When Mary graduates high school I could then go back to teaching school full-time. This is one area Jack is crazy about. He wants me to go back to school as a teacher now.

Jack: I know who is crazy, and it's not me. You decided to turn our family upside-down and you have to live with the results.

(I am being flooded with too much deep information too soon. While I know little about the couple's decision to divorce, I need to learn all that detracts them from true "Reasoned Decision-Making." This is also a tense period in the infancy of the mediation. Attacking words like "crazy" easily provokes defensive reactions. The interpersonal momentum can quickly deteriorate into a lack of trust in the process. Extreme care to "Restructure" their Momentum is needed, or one party will bail out emotionally, if not physically.)

Mediator: Susan, maybe you want to refrain from using the term "crazy" and tell me about your concerns about teaching full-time now. Jack, I promise I'll give you equal time to respond, okay? Jack nods.

Susan: This divorce has been very hard on the children. Jack is a workaholic who was a great provider, but never knew how to be a good parent. He is just like his own father. We tried to address this issue for years in counseling, but nothing worked. Thus, I have been "everything" for the children – disciplinarian, homework adviser, and bill payer. The kids have relied on me for this, and if I went back to school full-time I would never have time for them. Being an aide means I leave school at 2 p.m. and have time for them at night. If I was a teacher, I would have work to do on nights and weekends. Besides, I'll need a Master's degree to go back to full-time teaching in order to compete with the young teachers of today.

(I have temporarily corrected the communication pattern, but it must be monitored. Susan is now identifying her true, need-based concerns. It is my job to test her assumptions, but her tone is mature. Notice how often she uses the pronoun "I.")

Mediator: I see. (turning to Jack) How do you see the teaching issue Jack?

(I use the open-ended question to allow Jack to validate his concerns. The question controls the flow of Jack's concerns. Good open-ended questions must be carefully crafted by the questioner.)

Jack: I'm a good father. Yes, Susan did most of the homework, but I was always there for my kids. I took them to many of their ball games. I even have taken the kids to work with me sometimes to help Susan out.

Mediator: I see. Can I ask you, Jack how you see the school issue? Do you think the children need Susan more now given the changes in your family?

(I am asking him to test his own assumptions here. I am also hopefully stimulating Jack to consider the possible effects of the children spending less time with their mother.)

Jack: Look, they are not babies anymore. Julie has gone off to college. Jack Jr. will be leaving soon and Mary is almost a teenager. We are not talking about babies. Also, I have to get off my parents' couch, and get my own place. With the child support that I am paying I have very little left for myself. I want to see the children in my own place. Sue could make three times the money she makes now if she taught full-time.

Susan (interrupts Jack): You spend most nights at your girlfriend's. Let's be honest.

Jack (turning to Susan): This is what you wanted.

(I ponder whether these are simple statements, or do these statements reflect more unresolved feelings each has for one another.

Again, I must Restructure the Momentum as well as inquire into their true feelings.)

Mediator: Susan, please don't interrupt. I'll certainly listen to your position again. But Jack, I have to ask you since you mentioned it twice; are you unhappy over the breakup?

Jack: No; I mean I was at first, but our counseling convinced me that Susan did not love me anymore.

Mediator (I confront his somewhat illogical posture, given he has emotionally "moved on"): Then why do you still offer comments to Susan that this is all her fault?

Jack: I guess it's just a way of getting back at her. I agree it does not help us solve these problems. I am actually very happy in my new relationship.

Susan: And I am happy about that for you. We each deserve to be happy, and I was just not happy.

(I consider these comments the nectar of cooperation. Each side is revealing deep life-searing needs that are the foundation of a new kind of trust for one another. I want to nourish this trust and acknowledge their mature views on their relationship.)

Mediator: You are both to be commended for sharing such caring, yet vulnerable information for one another. Your children will rely on that mature care as they find their way as adults.

Each side nods without saying anything.

Mediator: It seems to me that one issue to be addressed is the legitimacy of Susan's being in the home for the children. I am not sure we know the answer yet, but I am convinced I can help you examine the issue more objectively. Susan, it might just be that the children are adjusting better than you think, and you could start rebuilding your career now. Jack, it might be that the children really do need Susan's presence now; that they are not yet ready emotionally for their roles as children of divorce, and all that entails.

(I am broaching the concept of Reasoned, Not Regretful decision-making here. Rather than a debate about homes or work schedules, the focus is on the true needs of the children. I have to

make sure the parties are ready for a change in their thinking. I have planted a mediation "seed"- the growth of which is persuasion.)
Both parties nod.

Mediator: Jack, let's begin this examination as to what is best for your children. Jack, what do you think the kids need now?

Jack: I want to get an apartment near the kids. It would allow me to spend more time with them, and help Susan get a job.
(Susan rolls her eyes to show disbelief. I question Susan on the nonverbal cue.)

Susan: He never spent a lot of time with the kids before. It was always work, work, work, and he was too tired to help them.

Jack (defensively): Susan, I had to work those hours to pay for all the things you wanted.
(I may have erred in my "planting". The momentum is negative and reactive. I must restructure the topic.)

Mediator (interrupting): Folks, rehashing over this issue does not help us move forward. Let me understand this work issue better. Would you say Jack that since the separation you have had more or less time with the children?

Jack: Less, but the time I have with them is better. Maybe the separation helped me to consider my relationship with the children. I seem to know more about their lives now.

Mediator: Susan, what do you think about the kids' relationship with their father now?

Susan: He does seem to take more of an interest in their activities.
(Notice how quickly we are again discussing real issues in a mature way.)

Jack: Yes, and I want to spend normal weekends with them like any father. I cannot do that at my parents' home!

Susan (to Mediator): What if the kids don't want to spend weekends with him?
(Her question to me indicates that she is ambivalent about this subject. She does not reject the idea outright, but part of her fears

the results of a mistake. I decide to "Redefine the Conflict" in their eyes. Rather than a test of wills on what is best, why not bring in an outside authority as a reference. Depending on the dispute such an outside authority may be an accountant, realtor, or economist. In mediation, such measurement of information is accepted, as it is an objective study by an expert. In this case, I could have a child psychologist be the objective resource.

Mediator: Perhaps we could have a mental health or school counselor talk to the children about this subject. It might just be that the children are handling this better than you think.

Susan: I could agree with that idea – I just want someone the kids trust.

Jack: It sounds fine to me.

Mediator: Why don't we move for now to the issue of Jack getting his own apartment? I know this issue ties into some of the financial issues. Are you both okay with discussing this?

(I am shifting the topic in order to "Read" their other conflicts, but obtain their consent first. It also helps to shift topics that are heated and return to them when more consensus creates positive momentum.)

Jack and Sue nod in assent.

Mediator: Jack, what are your goals regarding your living situation?

Jack: Look, I have to get out of my parents' home. The home is small, and my parents are uncomfortable even though they don't say anything.

Susan: I'm not stopping you from moving out.

Jack: Yes, you are! By the time I pay you and "Uncle Sam" I have about $400 dollars a week.

Susan: Come on Jack. You were always getting extra cash for side plumbing work.

(I have a conflict of sorts as this data is shared. Often an independent analysis of businesses in a divorce is made even before mediation begins. This is especially true in family businesses of this type where cash income is often hard to document. Frequently, however, the parties are the best source of data, since the finances are clear to both sides. Also, there are negative motivations not to pursue this issue too diligently. Both may have to pay fines to the government for unpaid taxes.)

Mediator: (I pursue this factual history to help them address this potential dilemma.) Jack, is that true?

Jack: First of all, I am turning down some of this work. That's what led to the divorce, and I really want to see the kids more. I will show her all of my tax records since the separation. I am going to need several thousand dollars for a first and last months' rent. I looked at an apartment in your neighborhood, Susan, that I loved. It's three bedrooms and all done over, but the rent is $2000 per month. How can I afford that?

Susan: You could move in with your girlfriend. She has a big place.

Jack: Then I would never see the kids overnight. You don't want that and I don't want that.

Susan: That's true. Why don't you just sell the summer cottage? No one goes there anymore. The kids don't like it in the middle of nowhere, and you don't even go anymore.

Jack: I don't know, Susan. That cottage has been in my family for years. It would kill my parents if I sold it.

Mediator: Jack, what are the benefits of keeping the cottage?

(I want to test Jack's interests. Does the home satisfy a vacation's need post-divorce, or is it an emotional need not to disappoint his parents?)

Jack: We really have outgrown the area, as it is quite rural and I don't like driving four hours to get there. It's just that my parents gave it to us as a gift.

Mediator: I suggest we adjourn this session and I am going to give you two tasks over the next week. Jack, I want you to talk to your parents about the summer cottage. Would they object to your selling it given the limited value to your family right now? It might also be a financial resource for your family. Sue, I am going to ask you to look at the apartment that Jack would like to obtain in your neighborhood. Consider its suitability for your children, and any advantages or disadvantages it might have for your children. I am also going to delve into some of the financial issues such as child support, education, and division of your property in the next session, okay?

Both Jack and Sue nod.

(I feel somewhat positive about the state of negotiations at this point. The parties, while holding disparate views as to their roles as parents and their children's needs, are emotionally mature. They both realize the marriage is over which is often an emotional roadblock for other parents who often say the marriage is over. This can lead to unreasonable positions whereby anger or ambivalence is masked as substantive needs. While their narratives still need monitoring, their interpersonal momentum is largely positive. They are both measuring their new roles as single parents and demonstrating reasonable concerns for their children's needs.

In "Reading the Conflict," they hold distinct views as to the children's needs. Sue has been the primary nurturer of the children in the past and wants to hold on to that role. The divorce seems to have awakened Jack on his failures as a parent, and he fears Sue won't open the familial cocoon she has built. This issue is a huge key in their ongoing lives. If Jack is sincere in his wishes, and his desire to live in the children's neighborhood rather than at his girlfriend's, this will benefit the family. More of Jack's sentiments must be unearthed in mediation. This is done for two reasons: (1) to help Jack honestly assess his own goals as a parent and give specifics as to his relationship with the children, and (2) for Susan to hear and reassess her own comfort with any changes.

Jack will be urged to give specific goals in his renewed relationship with the children: perhaps an hour of homework on his nights with Mary, or helping to coach Jack Jr.'s soccer team. Thus his sincerity is tested and Sue may reconsider her views. On the financial side, the key issues thus far are the viability of Sue's underemployment and how the cottage may help form their future lives. Susan recognizes the need to go back to full time teaching one day and may need more education to get that job. Jack sees the underemployment as the only way he can get back on his financial feet. That may or may not be true.)

RECONVENING THE MEDIATION

(I will begin to "Redefine the Conflict" in this session. Each parent currently views their problems in "win-lose" terms. If Susan has the children more, Jack will have the children less. In Reasoned Decision-Making, the problem is scrutinized from a superior angle. Perhaps the children's schedule will be disrupted but they may benefit more by a stronger male role model in their teenage years. Perhaps the children need more time with Susan, now given their emotional state, as part of the divorce. This is the problem that both parents will assess to make the wisest of choices for the children and themselves. To do so they will have to test fears and assumptions that each parent holds in order to amend his or her thinking.)

Mediator: So folks, how did each of you make out last week?

Susan: Well, I saw the apartment and I thought it was nice, but overpriced. How is he going to afford $2,000 per month?

Jack: I know it's a lot. But I think it is important that Jack and Mary have their own bedrooms. Each of them has important school years ahead.

Sue (sighing): I know.

Jack: My parents surprised me. They know I am hurting financially, and have no problem with my selling it.

Mediator: What do you think should happen to the money if you sell it?

Jack: If I have to keep paying $600 a week in child support, I'll need it to pay my bills.

Sue: All of it?

Jack: No, but a majority of it.

Mediator: Jack and Sue, how about if we saw this money as a way to achieve the goals you have both articulated for your children. Sue, you have mentioned that you need to get a Master's degree to get back to teaching full-time. How much do you think that would cost?

Sue: About $25,000.

Mediator: If you started courses in the fall, it would start that journey for you. If Jack lived in the neighborhood, he could watch the children that night.

Sue: That's true.

Mediator: At the same time you could watch Jack's parenting abilities. Should you see the children benefitting from the schedule, you could accelerate your education.

Sue nods.

Mediator: Jack, what do you think?

Jack: I like it. But I have to be able to live a little and have money to spend when I'm with the kids.

Mediator: That's where the cottage comes in. Look at the cottage as a bank for you both. You are in a partnership as far as your assets are concerned. At some point, all of your assets will be split 50/50. There is no need here for long term alimony one day. If you sell the house and put the money into a joint account, you can both draw down its value for your needs. You could draw some of the $600 child support order from this account and have more personal money. Sue, you could use the account for your education.

Jack: That would help, but what about the rest of the money?

Mediator: You could do periodic balancing of the account. Hopefully, with Jack Jr. and Sue's higher education coming, there would be some help for them there.

Jack: This would certainly let me get the apartment and have a life again. I like the idea of Sue's getting the degree, but I just wish she could reapply now for a position.

Sue: Jack, I'm not going to get rehired now. I need to get more training in educational technology. This plan would help me do that.

Mediator: And let you assess how the children are adjusting to less time with you.

Sue: I like the idea that we are in control of that.

(The problem is being Redefined as their own solution.)

Jack: I guess I can live with the plan as long as I receive assurance from Sue that she will not dally on obtaining her degree.

Mediator: Well, we can monitor that situation. I could always see the children at some point and help you assess how they are adapting. This could be the basis of Sue's increasing or decreasing her course load.

(Again, an outside reference often lends credibility to a dispute.)

Jack: I can live with that.

Sue: Me too.

CONCLUSION

No one will care more about Jack and Sue's three children than them; no attorney, judge, or mediator. Their investment in the result– healthy children—was not enough to make the wisest of decisions. Their journey for now, however, concluded with reasoned and not regretful decision-making.

In regretful decision-making this couple could have embarked on an unhealthy domestic battle. The children could have been emotionally scarred and forced to align with one parent or the other. I have witnessed such unreasoned decision-making. Years later, the adult children from such marriages have awful memories of their childhood and fragile relationships with each parent.

From afar, it is often easy to see good solutions for Jack and Sue. But in my opinion, such people in conflict know each other too well. They blame, rationalize, justify, and defend their decision-making. Under the guise of believing that they are "right" and the other side is "wrong," people can engage in domestic or civil wars. In either case, the bodies are damaged either physically or emotionally.

In this mediation, the problem was turned on its head. The solution was obvious – what decisions were best for this family structurally and financially. The problem was navigating the best pathways.

I hope you see the potential for Rocco's 4 R's as a practical roadmap to cooperation. As you see my steps often overlap or revert to another step as cooperation is easily derailed. Restructuring the interpersonal momentum is a constant with either a defensive parent or a defiant employer. One innocent comment can defeat cooperation in a receiver's mind that is wired to interpret information a certain way.

Reading the Conflict has to be reassessed constantly. In many geo-political disputes today, mediators have to measure the political fallout from any resolution as importantly as measuring any boundary. In the above mediation, Jack and Sue had to connect the financial aspects of the case to achieve the goal of fostering strong, post-divorce, parental ties.

Jack and Sue's case hopefully illustrates how the couple redefined the problem in their eyes. Sue had to be helped to see that the children could actually benefit from having a stronger relationship with their father. A method was also implemented that Jack could earn that trust by moving into the children's neighborhood.

Jack had to see that it just might be that the children did need their mother more than he thought. The problem again was redefined in his eyes thus a wise solution was to build a new parental schedule more carefully. Through communication, he was able to convince Sue that his financial obligations were limiting his ability to be a better parent.

The road to reasoned decision-making is never easy. But the alternative—regretful decision-making – is motivation to look for better interpersonal solutions.

Our lives are often littered with emotionally based reactive decisions that look so foolish in hindsight. All of us can slow down our reactions, apply reasoned steps, and seek good alternatives. Have a good journey!